Wynnere and Wastoure

and

The Parlement of the Thre Ages

Middle English Texts

General Editor

Russell A. Peck
University of Rochester

Advisory Board

Rita Copeland
University of Texas

Thomas G. Hahn
University of Rochester

Lisa Kiser
Ohio State University

Thomas Seiler
Western Michigan University

R. A. Shoaf
University of Florida

Bonnie Wheeler
Southern Methodist University

The Middle English Texts Series is designed for classroom use. Its goal is to make available to teachers and students texts which occupy an important place in the literary and cultural canon but which have not been readily available in student editions. The series does not include those authors such as Chaucer, Gower, Langland, the Pearl-poet, or Malory, whose English works are normally in print in good student editions. The focus is, instead, upon Middle English literature adjacent to those authors that teachers need in compiling the syllabuses they wish to teach. The editions maintain the linguistic integrity of the original work but within the parameters of modern reading conventions. The texts are printed in the modern alphabet and follow the practices of modern capitalization and punctuation. Manuscript abbreviations are expanded, and u/v and j/i spellings are regularized according to modern orthography. Hard words, difficult phrases, and unusual idioms are glossed on the page, either in the right margin or at the foot of the page. Textual notes appear at the end of the text, along with a glossary. The editions include short introductions on the history of the work, its merits and points of topical interest, and also include briefly annotated bibliographies.

Wynnere and Wastoure

and

The Parlement of the Thre Ages

Edited by

Warren Ginsberg

Published for TEAMS
(The Consortium for the Teaching of the Middle Ages)
in Association with the University of Rochester

by

Medieval Institute Publications

WESTERN MICHIGAN UNIVERSITY

Kalamazoo, Michigan — 1992

Library of Congress Cataloging-in-Publication Data

Wynnere and Wastoure
    Wynnere and Wastoure ; and, The Parlement of the thre ages /
edited by Warren Ginsberg.
        p.   cm. -- (Middle English texts)
    Includes bibliographical references.
    ISBN 1-879288-26-5 : $6.95
    1. Debate poetry, English (Middle) 2. Visions--Poetry.
  3. Dreams--Poetry.   I. Ginsberg, Warren, 1949- . II. Parlement
of the thre ages. 1992. III. Title. IV. Series: Middle English
texts (Kalamazoo, Mich.)
    PR2163.A2G56 1992
    821'.1--dc20   92-31284
                                                                         CIP

ISBN 1-879288-26-5

Copyright 1992 by the Board of the Medieval Institute

Printed in the United States of America

Cover design by Elizabeth King

Contents

Preface

In preparing this edition of *Wynnere and Wastoure* and *The Parlement of the Thre Ages* I have been aided by a grant from the Office of Research at the State University of New York at Albany, which allowed me to consult the manuscript and obtain a microfilm of it. I am grateful for this support.

I would like to thank Professor Russell A. Peck for his advice and his critique: both helped to make the edition better. I would like to thank Karen Saupe, Thomas H. Seiler, and Juleen Eichinger for their assistance in preparing camera-ready copy. And I would like to thank my wife, Judith Baskin, and our children, Sam and Shira, for their support as well: as always, they helped to unravel all that was tangled and, as always, they gave the straightforward a touch of wonder.

Wynnere and Wastoure
and
The Parlement of the Thre Ages

Introduction

The Parlement of the Thre Ages and *Wynnere and Wastoure* are the last two items in British Library Additional MS 31042, a miscellany of religious histories, verse romances, poems by John Lydgate, carols, and other devotional or ethical poems, all compiled by Robert Thornton, probably around 1450.[1] Thornton was a man of some prestige in Yorkshire; if, as seems likely, he copied these works for himself and his family, his collection is a good example of the fondness which the English middle class had for devotional literature and historical romance in the late Middle Ages.[2]

Thornton's version of *Wynnere and Wastoure* is unique; *The Parlement of the Thre Ages*, however, also exists in an incomplete and later, inferior version, which now is British Library Additional MS 33994 but formerly was part of the library of Sir James Ware, who died in 1666. Both *Wynnere* and *Parlement* share very nearly the same dialect; the language is that of the Midlands, though scholars disagree about its exact provenance. Suggested locations range from the North Central Midlands, possibly Nottinghamshire, to "somewhere not very far from where the counties of Yorkshire, Lincolnshire and Nottinghamshire meet," to the North-West Midlands, to the East

---

[1] For a discussion of Thornton and his manuscript, see George Keiser, "Lincoln Cathedral Library MS.91: Life and Milieu of the Scribe," *Studies in Bibliography* 32 (1979), 158–79; Keiser, "More Light on the Life and Milieu of Robert Thornton," *Studies in Bibliography* 36 (1983), 111–19; Ralph Hanna III, "The Growth of Robert Thornton's Books," *Studies in Bibiliography* 40 (1987), 51–61; and Stephanie Trigg, ed., *Wynnere and Wastoure*, EETS 297 (Oxford: Oxford University Press, 1990), introduction.

[2] See Trigg, ed., *Wynnere and Wastoure,* xvii; Anne Middleton, "The Audience and Public of *Piers Plowman*," in *Middle English Alliterative Poetry*, ed. David Lawton (Suffolk: Brewer, 1982), pp. 102–23; and Janet Coleman, *English Literature in History 1350–1400* (London: Hutchinson, 1981), pp. 13–67, on the kinds of literature the middle class read in late medieval England.

Midlands.[1] As a Northerner, Thornton sometimes introduces his own distinctive forms, just as the original poet accepted a number of Southern forms which had become part of the language of London. In any case, even if the locale of the language could be fixed precisely, the mixture of forms, as the most recent editor of *Wynnere and Wastoure* has said, suggests that this poet, like other writers of alliterative verse, was not isolated in the provinces but quite mobile (Trigg, p. xxii). When compared to other poems on contemporary issues, which tend to be "intensely provincial [and] hometown," *Wynnere and Wastoure* certainly seems national, even international in its outlook.[2] More than one might at first suppose, the dialect of *Wynnere* and *The Parlement of the Thre Ages* as well looks beyond narrow regionalism.

The close similarity of language and meter, in addition to the resemblances between Wynnere and Wastoure, in the poem bearing their names, and Medill Elde and Youthe, in *Parlement*, led the poems' first editor, Sir Israel Gollancz, to believe that they are by the same author. There is, however, no convincing evidence to support this conclusion; at most one can say with M. Y. Offord, who summarizes discussion of the question of authorship in her edition of *The Parlement of the Thre Ages*, that *Parlement* was composed by someone who spoke the same dialect as the poet of *Wynnere*.[3]

As for the date of the poems, the longstanding assumption has been that *Wynnere and Wastoure* was the earlier poem; just when *Wynnere* was composed, however, has provoked a great deal of controversy. *Wynnere* contains elements of topical satire; Gollancz in fact thought that it was aimed specifically at Edward III and the Black

---

[1] The quotation is from Angus McIntosh, "The Textual Transmission of the Alliterative *Morte Arthure*," in *English and Medieval Studies Presented to J. R. R. Tolkien,* ed. Norman Davis and C. L. Wrenn (London: Allen and Unwin, 1962), pp. 231–32. See Trigg, ed., *Wynnere and Wastoure,* for a summary of the literature that discusses the provenance of the poems' dialect.

[2] The quotation is from Rossell Hope Robbins, "Poems Dealing with Contemporary Conditions," in Albert Hartung, ed. *Manual of the Writings in Middle English 1050–1500* (New Haven: Connecticut Academy of Arts and Sciences, 1975), V, 1358.

[3] M. Y. Offord, ed., *The Parlement of the Thre Ages,* EETS 246 (Oxford: Oxford University Press, 1959), p. xxxvi. Offord goes on to claim that the poet of *Parlement* probably knew *Wynnere* well enough to imitate; this conclusion, however, is not based on the firmest of evidence. One correspondence relies on a highly suspect emendation of "sowrede" to "sowede" in *Wynnere,* line 215 (compare *Parlement* line 286); another compares *Parlement*'s "by-fore-with his eghne," line 549, to *Wynnere*'s "to-fore-with myn eghne," line 434. These compound prepositions are rare, but they are not identical, and the idiomatic character of the expression should be taken into account. The connection Offord sees between the poems affects her dating of *Parlement*.

Prince and their handling of events, both foreign and domestic, during the winter of 1352–53. The poem does indeed seem to comment on economic and political conditions in the wake of the Black Death, which struck England in 1348–49. Labor was in short supply in the years following the plague's outbreak, and many workers would break contracts and journey to wherever wages were highest; at the same time, bands of criminals, not only of the lower classes but of the urban and country gentry as well, were causing alarming mayhem.[1] Parliament passed a number of measures in response; among the most important were The Statute of Laborers in 1351 and The Statute of Treasons in 1352.[2] Both these laws, but especially the former, created a great deal of resentment, some of which was directed at William Shareshull (prominently mentioned in the poem at line 317), who as Chief Justice was instrumental in their promulgation.[3] In fact, Wastoure's vehement denial that he has disturbed the peace (lines 317–18) has been taken to refer both to the Treasons Statute and to an uprising in Chester in 1353 (the only insurrection to have occurred in the West between 1349 and 1365), which Shareshull had a part in provoking. But the conditions these acts of Parliament addressed persisted at least until Shareshull died in 1370, which establishes a fairly certain *terminus ad quem* for the poem; for a *terminus a quo*, the best we can say is that *Wynnere*, which does seem to allude to the Statute of Treasons (in lines 126ff.), was probably not composed earlier than 1352.[4]

Similarly, nothing about the situation abroad can help to determine the date with greater precision. *Wynnere* does reflect how dependent Edward III had become on merchants to finance his expeditions in France during The Hundred Years' War.

---

[1] See May McKisack, *The Fourteenth Century 1307–1399* (Oxford: Clarendon, 1959), pp. 204–07, for an account of these gangs.

[2] One should note that criminal activity was part of the fabric of life in England throughout the Middle Ages. While the Statute of Treasons was certainly an attempt to conserve law and order, it was by no means unique; in fact, judging from the documents, lawlessness did not increase dramatically in the years immediately following the plague. See Richard Kaeuper, *War, Justice and Public Order: England and France in the Later Middle Ages* (Oxford: Clarendon, 1988), pp. 170–83.

[3] The chief provisions of the Statute of Laborers fixed wages at pre-plague rates, ordered all landless men under sixty years of age to accept employment at these rates, and mandated that their lords were to have first claim on their services. For some years after 1351, attempts to enforce the law were vigorous and largely successful (McKisack, *The Fourteenth Century,* p. 335). On the Statute of Treasons, see below, note to *Wynnere,* lines 130ff.

[4] For a full discussion of the debate over the date of the poem, see Trigg, pp. xxii–xxvii. As an absolute *terminus a quo,* the motto of the Order of the Garter is translated in the poem; Edward III instituted the Order in 1349.

Indeed, to raise money without Parliament's involvement, Edward had even tried to form an Estate of Merchants; this group played so important a part in the parliaments of 1352–54, it began to rival the Commons.[1] But the war with France commanded Edward's attention until his death; both he and Richard II after him depended on merchants throughout the rest of the fourteenth century. There is little to prove that the poem's descriptions refer specifically to Edward's campaign in 1353.

The Parlement of the Thre Ages, however, is not topical; nothing in it can allow fixing a date more definite than between 1352–53 and about 1390. Offord thinks it probable that the poem was composed before 1370, but acknowledges this as supposition. Indeed, she points out that we cannot even be sure that *Wynnere* did in fact precede *The Parlement.* In the end, arguments for placing one poem before the other rest more on editorial ideas of evolution than on the data of the works; in this the relationship between *Wynnere and Wastoure* and *The Parlement of the Thre Ages* echoes the recent discussions on the development of alliterative poetry in Middle English in general. Influence cannot be determined with certainty.[2]

In both *Wynnere and Wastoure* and *The Parlement of the Thre Ages,* a solitary narrator falls asleep and witnesses in his dream a verbal altercation about current social abuses and defects of the spirit. The poems are thus complaints that combine at least two medieval genres, the dream vision and the poetic debate: much critical commentary has sought to elucidate how generic expectations are met or modified in each poem.

That both poems have produced interpretations quite at odds with one another is not surprising, since both dream visions and the poetic debate have venerable and complicated histories. The purpose of each was to teach, yet from the start both also called into question the certainty of their instruction and the degree to which we can rely on the person who gives or receives it. Dreams could carry the authority of

---

[1] See John V. Scattergood, *"Wynnere and Wastoure* and the Mid-Fourteenth Century Economy," in *The Writer as Witness: Literature as Historical Evidence,* ed. Tom Dunne (Cork: Cork University Press, 1987), p. 52.

[2] The presumed early date of *Wynnere* especially has figured largely in accounts of Middle English alliterative poetry. Because *Wynnere* is technically sophisticated, critics have postulated that earlier, less accomplished alliterative poems existed but have been lost. John Burrow, for instance ("The Audience of Piers Plowman," *Anglia* 75 [1957], 373–84), has thought that in an effort to make *Piers Plowman* more accessible to Londoners, Langland specifically tempered the excesses in alliterative style and vocabulary of *Wynnere.* More recently, however, David Lawton has argued that it is equally possible, based on the evidence, to argue that *Wynnere* was influenced by *Piers.*

divine revelation or be the unreliable products of wish fulfillment.[1] Debates could resolve the issue under question decisively or leave it in doubt.[2] As a consequence, suspicions about the reliability of the dreamer or disputants could readily be entertained, even when the wisdom of what they said seemed unimpeachable.

Moreover, the prologues of both poems have much in common with the traditional "chanson d'aventure," in which a narrator, wandering alone, hears a bird-song, or meets a lady, or reads a message on a wall, or overhears a complaint or debate. As Anne Middleton says, the speaker "happens on truth or transformation unawares, in a place, time and state of mind where it was least looked for" (p. 114). Consequently, a "poem in this mode does not present authoritative truth to cognition . . . its definitive features are that its speaker has no authority and that the truth of its discourse is purely contingent" (pp. 114–15).

In *Wynnere and Wastoure* and *The Parlement of the Thre Ages*, therefore, generic affiliations multiply rather than simplify the complexities of interpretation even before we discover the particular concerns of each poem. In *Wynnere*, for instance, it is hard to decide which combatant should win the debate; the manuscript ends before the king can complete his determination, and what he does say, considering that he himself both wins and wastes, leaves the argument between getting and spending appropriately unresolved. The poem's perspectives are truly dizzying: on the one hand, economics, politics, ethics, and social relations are seen as an interrelated set of universal, timeless principles; on the other, they appear as actual, contingent conditions that have resulted from specific acts in history. As allegorical personifications, Wynnere attempts to portray himself as desirable gain and Wastoure as sheer Prodigality; Wastoure in turn pictures Wynnere as pure Avarice and himself as efficacious expenditure. Their altercation inevitably recalls Aristotle's ethical axiom that liberality, which is the mean between the excesses of both vices, is the proper guide to conduct. But Wynnere and Wastoure debate before the king: at times their arguments seem less philosophical and more a pointed comment on the constant tension between the two main departments of Edward III's household. The lord

---

[1] For a convenient summary of the range of meaning dreams had in the Middle Ages, see A. C. Spearing, *Medieval Dream Poetry* (Cambridge: Cambridge University Press, 1976), pp. 1–24.

[2] Academic disputations, legal argumentation in the courts, and parliamentary debate form the institutional context of the poetic debate in Middle English: see Thomas Reed, *Middle English Debate Poetry and the Aesthetics of Irresolution* (Columbia and London: University of Missouri Press, 1990), for an up-to-date survey; and John W. Conlee, *Middle English Debate Poetry: A Critical Anthology* (East Lansing: Colleagues Press, 1991), for numerous examples.

5

chamberlain was responsible for outlays that guaranteed, as one source puts it, the "king's magnificence"; the lord steward was responsible for the actual running of the king's household and insuring his "providence."[1] Yet Edward's need for money to make war in France also gave his domestic affairs a larger political dimension: in Simon Islip's *De Speculo Regis Edwardi III*, for instance, he is called "avarus," an avaricious man, and "prodigus," because of his abuse of purveyance to raise money and because of the extravagancy of his household expenses.[2] Then again, some of Wastoure's barbs against Wynnere show that the rising status of merchants was a real cause for concern among those who still believed in the sanctioned social hierarchy. And so it goes: in each of the four exchanges between Wynnere and Wastoure the universal is set alongside the particular, as specific economic, political, and social disorders are condemned by appealing to ethical and religious ideals. To try to follow their debate, much less to resolve it, without invoking a multitude of perspectives seems as doomed to partiality as are Wynnere's and Wastoure's own arguments.

In *The Parlement of the Thre Ages*, religious and moral standards are invoked to highlight the degradation of social abuses in a somewhat different way; consequently, problems of interpretation have taken a different form. Older studies (e.g., Speirs and Everett) commended the lively realism of *The Parlement of the Thre Ages*, especially the descriptions of the hunt and the brittling of the deer, but faulted the lack of proportion they saw in its construction. To them, little connects the prologue with the debate that follows it, and Elde's disquisition on the Nine Worthies was over-long in itself and not relevant to the issues about which Youthe, Medill Elde, and Elde quarrel. More recently, however, a number of studies have argued that the poet carefully anticipates the argument of the dream in the hunt of the prologue (e.g., Peck and Lampe), and that Elde's speech does in fact address and effectively answer both Youthe and Medill Elde (e.g., Kiser). The grave battles of the Nine Worthies, for instance, set Youthe's penchant for tournaments in sober context; so too does Medill Elde's preoccupation with land and control of his household seem small and misconceived when one considers that the Worthies possessed and ruled the entire world yet lost everything when they died.

But even if we grant that Elde effectively silences Youthe and Medill Elde and thereby wins the debate, he himself nonetheless seems self-involved and given to the

---

[1] On the king's "familia," see Richard F. Green, *Poets and Princepleasers* (Toronto: University of Toronto Press, 1981); for a reading of *Wynnere and Wastoure* in terms of the king's household, see David Starkey, "The Age of the Household: Politics, Society and the Arts, *c.* 1350 – *c.* 1550," in *The Later Middle Ages,* ed. Stephen Medcalf (London: Methuen, 1981), pp. 253–58.

[2] See Scattergood, *"Wynnere and Wastoure,"* p. 48.

vices of old age. Elde shows that in the face of death the extravagance of youth and the industry of middle age are equally vain, yet the very decisiveness of the answer prompts a further question. How can a character able to formulate such commendable truths still be given to anger and envy (line 163)?

For this edition, only a highly simplified discussion of the poems' meter is appropriate.[1] The most common type of line has four or five main stresses, three of which alliterate. All lines have a break somewhere mid-line; the half-line that follows the break is usually shorter and contains at least two stresses. Consonants alliterate with themselves, as do certain groups of consonants (e.g., *sp, st, sw*).[2] Any vowel alliterates with any other vowel and, in *Parlement* (but *not* in *Wynnere*), with mute "h" in words of French origin (*herbere — anone — aftir, Parlement* line 74).

Alliterating stresses fall into numerous patterns. By far the most common is *aa/ax*. There are many variations: the one I will comment on here, because it affects the editing of the text, is the pattern *aa/xx*. The most recent editor of *Wynnere*, Stephanie Trigg, does not accept this pattern unless a number of conditions are met. I, however, accept it throughout for two reasons. First, *Wynnere* itself provides too small a statistical sample to be certain that the poet did not allow this pattern. Second, if one expands one's base and takes *The Parlement* into account, one finds that the pattern *aa/xx* occurs sixteen times in this poem, frequently enough to make Offord say that the poet may indeed have recognized the type.[3] Even if the poems are by different authors, their metrics in other respects are close enough to conclude that emending the text to remedy an otherwise acceptable line of the *aa/xx* type does not seem warranted.

For this edition, I have followed the guidelines of the Middle English Text Series in printing the modern equivalents of thorns, edhs, and yoghs, and in rationalizing the distribution of i/j and u/v in accordance with modern spellings. All abbreviations have been silently expanded, with one notable exception: in words with medial -n- or

---

[1] Both Trigg and Offord have full discussions of meter in their editions; Offord's is more traditional and relies on knowledge of Old English metrics; Trigg's is up-to-date, but polemical in the sense that it offers a justificiation for her emendations on metrical grounds.

[2] Other groups vary: *sl* sometimes alliterates with itself, sometimes with *s*; other combinations such as *fl* or *fr* are not considered groups at all.

[3] Offord, ed., *The Parlement of the Thre Ages,* p. xxxii. The instances in *Parlement* also in large measure fall outside the conditions (couplet alliteration and voiced and unvoiced consonant alliteration) which make the pattern acceptable to Trigg.

-m-, it is seldom clear how or whether to expand the curved stroke that often appears above it. I have therefore ignored it throughout. The division into paragraphs follows the MS, where divisions are indicated by a large capital. The text is heavily glossed; unfamiliar words that have not been regularly glossed after their third occurrence appear in the glossary.

Although I have had the advantage of being able to consult two fine editions, Trigg's of *Wynnere and Wastoure* and Offord's of *The Parlement of the Thre Ages*, I have nevertheless established the text of each poem by consulting the manuscript itself and a microfilm of it. All emended readings are discussed in the notes.

Select Bibliography

Editions

Burrow, John A., ed. *English Verse 1300–1500*. London: Longman, 1977. [Excerpt of *Wynnere*.]

Gollancz, Israel, ed. *The Parlement of the Thre Ages*. London: Oxford University Press, 1915.

———, ed. *A Good Short Debate between Winner and Waster*. Oxford, 1921; rpt. Cambridge: Brewer, 1974.

Offord, M. Y., ed. *The Parlement of the Thre Ages*. EETS 246. Oxford: Oxford University Press, 1959.

Trigg, Stephanie, ed. *Wynnere and Wastoure*. EETS 297. Oxford: Oxford University Press, 1990.

Turville-Petre, Thorlac. "An Anthology of Medieval Poems and Drama." In *Medieval Literature: Chaucer and the Alliterative Tradition*, ed. Boris Ford. *New Pelican Guide to English Literature*, I, pt. 1. Harmondsworth: Penguin, 1982. [*Wynnere* only.]

———. *Alliterative Poetry of the Later Middle Ages: An Anthology*. Washington, D.C.: Catholic University of America Press, 1989. [Includes both *Wynnere* and *Parlement*, pp. 38–100.]

Introduction

General and Comparative Studies

Burrow, John A. *The Ages of Man*. Oxford: Clarendon, 1988.

Coleman, Janet. *English Literature in History 1350–1400*. London: Hutchinson, 1981.

Hanna, Ralph III. "The Growth of Robert Thornton's Books." *Studies in Bibliography* 40 (1987), 51–61.

Harrington, David V. "Indeterminacy in *Winner and Waster* and *The Parliament of the Three Ages*." *Chaucer Review* 20 (1986), 246–57.

Hieatt, Constance. "*Wynnere and Wastoure* and *The Parlement of the Thre Ages*." *American Notes and Queries* 4 (1966), 100–04.

Keiser, George. "Lincoln Cathedral Library MS.91: Life and Milieu of the Scribe." *Studies in Bibliography* 32 (1979), 158–79.

———. "More Light on the Life and Milieu of Robert Thornton." *Studies in Bibliography* 36 (1983), 111–19.

Lawton, David. "Literary History and Scholarly Fancy: The Date of Two Middle English Alliterative Poems." *Parergon* 18 (1977), 17–25.

Middleton, Anne. "The Audience and Public of *Piers Plowman*." In *Middle English Alliterative Poetry*, ed. David Lawton (Suffolk: Brewer, 1982), pp. 101–23.

Oakden, James P. *Alliterative Poetry in Middle English*. Vol. 2. Manchester: Manchester University Press, 1935.

Reed, Thomas L., Jr. *Middle English Debate Poetry and the Aesthetics of Irresolution*. Columbia and London: University of Missouri Press, 1990.

Spearing, Anthony C. *Medieval Dream Poetry*. Cambridge: Cambridge University Press, 1976.

Speirs, John. "*Wynnere and Wastoure* and *The Parlement of the Thre Ages*." *Scrutiny* 17 (1950), 241–49. Rpt. in *Medieval English Poetry: The Non-Chaucerian Tradition*. London: Faber and Faber, 1957.

Steadman, John M., Jr. "The Authorship of *Wynnere and Wastoure* and *The Parlement of the Thre Ages*: A Study in Methods of Determining the Common Authorship of Middle English Poems." *Modern Philology* 21 (1923), 7–13.

Starkey, David. "The Age of the Household: Politics, Society and the Arts, *c.* 1350–*c.* 1550." In Stephen Medcalf, ed., *The Later Middle Ages* (London: Methuen, 1981), pp. 225–90.

Utley, Francis Lee. "Dialogues, Debates, and Catechisms." In *A Manual of the Writings in Middle English, 1050–1500*, ed. Albert E. Hartung (New Haven: Connecticut Academy of Arts and Sciences, 1972), III, 669–745, 829–902.

Vale, Juliet. *Edward III and Chivalry: Chivalric Society and its Context 1270–1350*. Cambridge: The Boydell Press, 1982.

Wynnere and Wastoure

Anderson, Jesse M. "A Note on the Date of *Winnere and Wastoure*." *Modern Language Notes* 43 (1928), 47–49.

Bestul, Thomas. *Satire and Allegory in Wynnere and Wastoure*. Lincoln: University of Nebraska Press, 1974.

Elliott, R. W. V. "The Topography of *Wynnere and Wastoure*." *English Studies* 48 (1967), 134–40.

Ginsberg, Warren. "Place and Dialectic in Dante's *Paradiso* and the Middle English *Pearl*." *English Literary History* 55 (1989), 731–53.

Havely, Nicholas. "The Dominicans and Their Banner in *Wynnere and Wastoure*." *Notes and Queries, n.s.* 30 (1983), 207–09.

Hulbert, James R. "The Problems of Authorship and Date of *Wynnere and Wastoure*." *Modern Philology* 18 (1920), 31–40.

Jacobs, Nicolas. "The Typology of Debate and the Interpretation of *Wynnere and Wastoure*." *Review of English Studies* 36 (1985), 481–500.

James, Jerry D. "The Undercutting of Conventions in *Wynnere and Wastoure*." *Modern Language Quarterly* 25 (1964), 243–58.

Moran, D. V. "*Wynnere and Wastoure*: An Extended Footnote." *Neuphilologische Mitteilungen* 73 (1972), 683–85.

Oiji, Takero. "An Essay on *Wynnere and Wastoure*, with Special Reference to the Political, Economic and Religious Attitudes of the Poet." *Studies in English Literature* (Tokyo) 43 (1966), 1–14. [In Japanese: English summary, 127–28.]

Salter, Elizabeth. "The Timeliness of *Wynnere and Wastoure*." *Medium Aevum* 47 (1978), 40–65.

Scattergood, John V. "*Wynnere and Wastoure* and the Mid-Fourteenth Century Economy." In *The Writer as Witness: Literature as Historical Evidence*, ed. Tom Dunne (Cork: Cork University Press, 1987), pp. 39–57.

Steadman, John M., Jr. "The Date of "*Wynnere and Wastoure*." *Modern Philology* 19 (1921), 211–19.

Turville-Petre, Thorlac. "The Prologue of *Wynnere and Wastoure*." *Leeds Studies in English* 19 (1987), 19–29.

The Parlement of the Thre Ages

Coffman, George R. "Old Age from Horace to Chaucer." *Speculum* 9 (1934), 249–77.

Everett, Dorothy. *Essays on Middle English Literature*, ed. Patricia Kean (Oxford: Clarendon, 1959), pp. 51–52.

Kernan, Anne. "Theme and Structure in *The Parlement of the Thre Ages*." *Neuphilologische Mitteilungen* 75 (1974), 253–78.

Kiser, Lisa. "Elde and His Teaching in *The Parlement of the Thre Ages*." *Philological Quarterly* 66 (1987), 303–14.

Lampe, David. "The Poetic Strategy of *The Parlement of the Thre Ages*." *Chaucer Review* 7 (1973), 173–83.

Lewis, Robert E. "The Date of *The Parlement of the Thre Ages*." *Neuphilologische Mitteilungen* 69 (1968), 380–90.

Moran, Dennis. "*The Parlement of the Thre Ages*: Meaning and Design." *Neophilologus* 62 (1978), 620–33.

Peck, Russell A. "The Careful Hunter in *The Parlement of the Thre Ages*." *English Literary History* 39 (1972), 333–41.

Rowland, Beryl. "The Three Ages of *The Parlement of the Thre Ages*." *Chaucer Review* 9 (1975), 342–52.

Scattergood, John. "*The Parlement of the Thre Ages*." *Leeds Studies in English* 14 (1983), 167–81.

Shibata, Yoshitaka. "An Essay on *The Parlement of the Thre Ages*." *Journal of the English Institute* 13 (1984), 1–26. [In Japanese: English summary, 24.]

Turville-Petre, Thorlac. "The Ages of Man in *The Parlement of the Thre Ages*." *Medium Aevum* 46 (1977), 66–76.

———. "The Nine Worthies in *The Parlement of the Thre Ages*." *Poetica* 11 (1979), 28–45.

Waldron, R. A. "The Prologue to *The Parlement of the Thre Ages*." *Neuphilologische Mitteilungen* 73 (1972), 786–94.

Whitney, Carol Wilkinson. "The Hunted Hunter of the *Alliterative Morte Arthure*." *Mediaevalia* 14 (1988), 179–99.

Wynnere and Wastoure

Here begynnes a tretys and god schorte refreyte bytwixe Wynnere and Wastoure[1]

	Sythen that Bretayne was biggede and Bruyttus it aughte,	
	Thurgh the takynge of Troye with tresone withinn,[2]	
	There hathe selcouthes bene sene in seere kynges tymes,	*marvels; various*
	Bot never so many as nowe by the nyne dele.	*ninth part*
5	For nowe alle es witt and wyles that we with delyn,	*deal with*
	Wyse wordes and slee, and icheon wryeth othere.[3]	
	Dare never no westren wy while this werlde lasteth	*western man*
	Send his sone southewarde to see ne to here,	*nor to hear*
	That he ne schall holden byhynde when he hore eldes.[4]	
10	Forthi sayde was a sawe of Salomon the wyse —	*Therefore; saying*
	It hyeghte harde appone honde, hope I no nother —	*hastens*
	When wawes waxen schall wilde and walles bene doun,	*waves*
	And hares appon herthe-stones schall hurcle in hire fourme,[5]	
	And eke boyes of blode with boste and with pryde,	*spirited low-born man*
15	Schall wedde ladyes in londe and lede hem at will,	*marry*
	Thene dredfull Domesdaye it draweth neghe aftir.	*Judgment Day; near*
	Bot whoso sadly will see and the sothe telle,	*seriously; truth*
	Say it newely will neghe or es neghe here.	*Say it will come soon*
	Whylome were lordes in londe that loved in thaire hertis	*Once*
20	To here makers of myrthes that matirs couthe fynde,	*hear*
	And now es no frenchipe in fere bot fayntnesse of hert,	*among companions*
	Wyse wordes withinn that wroghte were never,	*were never performed*
	Ne redde in no romance that ever renke herde.	*man*

---

[1] *Here begins a treatise and good short debate between Winner and Waster*

[2] *Lines 1–2: Since Britain was settled after Brutus had conquered it, / Following the destruction of Troy because of internal treason*

[3] *Wise words and subtle, and each word obscures the next (or, hides another intention)*

[4] *Because he (the son) shall not stay behind (i.e., at home) when he (the father) grows old and gray*

[5] *And hares shall crouch upon hearthstones for their lairs*

	Bot now a childe appon chere, withowtten chyn-wedys,	*face; beard*
25	That never wroghte thurgh witt thies wordes togedire,	*shaped*
	Fro he can jangle als a jaye and japes telle,	*knows how to; jokes*
	He schall be levede and lovede and lett of a while	*believed; esteemed for*
	Wele more than the man that made it hymselven.	*composed the poem*
	Bot, never-the-lattere, at the laste when ledys bene knawen,	
30	Werke wittnesse will bere who wirche kane beste. [1]	

[Fitt I]

	Bot I schall tell yow a tale that me bytyde ones	*happened to me*
	Als I went in the weste, wandrynge myn one,	*by myself*
	Bi a bonke of a bourne; bryghte was the sone	*bank; stream*
	Undir a worthiliche wodde by a wale medewe:	*lovely wood; pleasant*
35	Fele floures gan folde ther my fote steppede.	*Many; unfold where*
	I layde myn hede one ane hill ane hawthorne besyde;	
	The throstills full throly they threpen togedire,	*vigorously; contend in song*
	Hipped up heghwalles fro heselis tyll othire,	*Leapt; woodpeckers; hazel trees*
	Bernacles with thayre billes one barkes thay roungen, [2]	
40	The jay janglede one heghe, jarmede the foles.	*on high; the birds chirped*
	The bourne full bremly rane the bankes bytwene;	*stream; quickly ran*
	So ruyde were the roughe stremys and raughten so heghe [3]	
	That it was neghande nyghte or I nappe myghte,	*approaching; before*
	For dyn of the depe watir and dadillyng of fewllys.	*chattering; birds*
45	Bot as I laye at the laste than lowked myn eghne,	*closed; eyes*
	And I was swythe in a sweven sweped belyve.	*swiftly; dream swept at once*
	Me thoghte I was in the werlde, I ne wiste in whate ende,	*never knew*
	One a loveliche lande that was ylike grene,	*glade*
	That laye loken by a lawe the lengthe of a myle.	*enclosed by earthworks*
50	In aythere holte was ane here in hawberkes full brighte,	*army*
	Harde hattes appon hedes and helmys with crestys;	
	Brayden owte thaire baners, bown for to mete,	*They unfurled; ready*

---

[1] *Lines 29–30: But nevertheless, at the end, when men are revealed for what they are / Work will bear witness to those who know how to work best*

[2] *Barnacle geese with their beaks make a ringing sound on the bark of trees (or, peck noisily at their shells)*

[3] *So riotous were the rough streams that made so much noise (reached so far)*

Schowen owte of the schawes, in schiltrons thay felle, [1]
And bot the lengthe of a launde thies lordes bytwene.   *glade*
55 And alle prayed for the pese till the prynce come,
For he was worthiere in witt than any wy ells   *man else*
For to ridde and to rede and to rewlyn the wrothe   *advise; rule; anger*
That aythere here appon hate had untill othere. [2]
At the creste of a clyffe a caban was rerede,
60 Alle raylede with rede the rofe and the sydes,   *adorned; red; roof*
With Ynglysse besantes full brighte, betyn of golde,   *decorative coins; beaten*
And ichone gayly umbygone with garters of inde, [3]
And iche a gartare of golde gerede full riche.   *each; adorned*
Then were ther wordes in the webbe werped of he,   *woven up high*
65 Payntted of plunket, and poyntes bytwene,   *light blue; dots*
That were fourmed full fayre appon fresche lettres,
And alle was it one sawe appon Ynglysse tonge,   *a saying*
"Hethyng have the hathell that any harme thynkes."   *Shame; knight; slander*

Now the kyng of this kythe kepe hym oure Lorde!   *country*
70 Upon heghe one the holt ane hathell up stondes, [4]
Wroghte als a wodwyse alle in wrethyn lokkes, [5]
With ane helme one his hede, ane hatte appon lofte,   *helmet; cap*
And one heghe one the hatte ane hattfull beste,   *wrathful beast*
A lighte lebarde and a longe, lokande full kene,   *fierce*
75 Yarked alle of yalowe golde in full yape wyse.   *Made; skillful manner*
Bot that that hillede the helme byhynde in the nekke   *that which covered*
Was casten full clenly in quarters foure: *devised; skillfully*
Two with flowres of Fraunce before and behynde,   *above; below*
And two out of Ynglonde with sex grym bestes,   *six; beasts*
80 Thre leberdes one lofte and thre on lowe undir;   *above; below*
At iche a cornere a knoppe of full clene perle,   *stud*
Tasselde of tuly silke, tuttynge out fayre.   *red; projecting*
And by the cabane I knewe the knyghte that I see,

---

[1] *Pushed forward out of the woods, in phalanxes they deployed*

[2] *That either army in hatred had for the other*

[3] *And each one gaily surrounded with fastenings of blue*

[4] *High upon a wooded hill (or possibly stronghold, used figuratively) a nobleman stands up*

[5] *Dressed as a savage man of the wood (see note) in twisted tufts of fur*

15

	And thoghte to wiete or I went wondres ynewe.	*discover before; enough*
85	And als I waytted withinn I was warre sone	*looked inside; aware immediately*
	Of a comliche kynge crowned with golde,	
	Sett one a silken bynche, with septure in honde,	*throne*
	One of the lovelyeste ledis, whoso loveth hym in hert,	*of men*
	That ever segge under sonn sawe with his eghne.	*man; eyes*
90	This kynge was comliche clade in kirtill and mantill —	*tunic; sleeveless robe*
	Bery-brown was his berde — brouderde with fewlys,[1]	
	Fawkons of fyne golde, flakerande with wynges,	*flapping*
	And ichone bare in ble blewe als me thoghte	*bore; color*
	A grete gartare of ynde gerede full riche.	*decorated*
95	Full gayly was that grete lorde girde in the myddis:	
	A brighte belte of ble broudirde with fewles,	*color*
	With drakes and with dukkes — daderande tham semede	*trembling*
	For ferdnes of fawkons fete, lesse fawked thay were.	*terror; lest captured*
	And ever I sayd to myselfe, "Full selly me thynke	*marvelous*
100	Bot if this renke to the revere ryde umbestonde."	*knight; river; sometimes*
	The kyng biddith a beryn by hym that stondeth,	*speaks to; knight*
	One of the ferlyeste frekes that faylede hym never:	*most marvelous men*
	"Thynke I dubbede the knyghte with dynttis to dele!	*you; blows*
	Wende wightly thy waye my willes to kythe.	*quickly; make known*
105	Go, bidd thou yondere bolde batell that one the bent hoves,[2]	
	That they never neghe nerre togedirs;	*come nearer*
	For if thay strike one stroke stynte thay ne thynken."	*stop*
	"Yis, lorde," said the lede, "while my life dures."	*man*
	He dothe hym doun one the bonke, and dwellys awhile	*goes*
110	Whils he busked and bown was one his beste wyse.	*dressed; equipped*
	He laped his legges in yren to the lawe bones,	*enclosed; iron; lower*
	With pysayne and with pawnce polischede full clene,[3]	
	With brases of broun stele brauden full thikke,[4]	
	With plates buklede at the bakke the body to yeme,	*protect*
115	With a jupown full juste joynede by the sydes,[5]	

---

[1] *The king's beard was berry-brown (see note) — embroidered with birds*

[2] *Go, tell the bold warriors over yonder who await on the battlefield*

[3] *With neck armor and armor covering the stomach polished very shinily*

[4] *With pieces of armor for the arms of bright steel linked very tightly*

[5] *With a well-fitting tunic fastened at the sides*

A brod chechun at the bakke; the breste had another,   *escutcheon*

Thre wynges inwith wroghte in the kynde,   *wrought in a natural fashion*

Umbygon with a gold wyre. When I that gome knewe,   *Surrounded; man*

What! he was yongeste of yeris and yapeste of witt   *Lo; cleverest*

120   That any wy in this werlde wiste of his age.   *man; knew*

He brake a braunche in his hande, and caughte it swythe,   *swiftly*

Trynes one a grete trotte and takes his waye   *Goes*

There bothe thies ferdes folke in the felde hoves.   *armies'; wait*

Sayd, "Loo! the kyng of this kyth, ther kepe hym oure Lorde!   *country*

125   Send his erande by me, als hym beste lyketh,   *Sends his message (see note)*

That no beryn be so bolde, one bothe his two eghne,

Ones to strike one stroke, no stirre none nerre   *Once; nor (see note)*

To lede rowte in his rewme, so ryall to thynke   *troop; kingly*

Pertly with youre powers his pese to disturbe.   *Openly; peace*

130   For this es the usage here and ever schall worthe: *be*

If any beryn be so bolde with banere for to ryde

Withinn the kyngdome riche bot the kynge one,   *alone*

That he schall losse the londe and his lyfe aftir.

Bot sen ye knowe noghte this kythe ne the kynge ryche,   *kingdom*

135   He will forgiffe yow this gilt of his grace one.   *alone*

Full wyde hafe I walked amonges thies wyes one,   *among these people*

Bot sawe I never siche a syghte, segge, with myn eghne;   *sir*

For here es all the folke of Fraunce ferdede besyde,   *assembled*

Of Lorreyne, of Lumbardye, and of Lawe Spayne;

140   Wyes of Westwale, that in were duellen;   *Men; Westphalia; war*

Of Ynglonde, of Yrlonde, Estirlynges full many,   *Hanseatic merchants*

That are stuffede in stele, strokes to dele.

And yondere a banere of blake that one the bent hoves,   *battlefield waits*

With thre bulles of ble white brouden withinn,[1]

145   And iche one hase of henppe hynged a corde,   *a cord of hemp hanging down*

Seled with a sade lede; I say als me thynkes,   *heavy lead seal*

That hede es of holy kirke I hope he be there,[2]

Alle ferse to the fighte with the folke that he ledis.

Another banere es upbrayde with a bende of grene,   *unfurled; diagonal band*

---

[1] *With three papal bulls of white color embroidered within it*

[2] *That he who is head of Holy Church, I believe he is there*

17

150   With thre hedis white-herede with howes one lofte,   *lawyers' caps above them*

        Croked full craftyly and kembid in the nekke: *Curled*

        Thies are ledis of this londe that schold oure lawes yeme,   *protect*

        That thynken to dele this daye with dynttis full many.

        I holde hym bot a fole that fightis whils flyttynge may helpe,

155   When he hase founden his frende that fayled hym never. [1]

        The thirde banere one bent es of blee whitte,

        With sexe galegs, I see, of sable withinn,   *sandals; black*

        And iche one has a brown brase with bokels twayne.   *strap*

        Thies are Sayn Franceys folke, that sayen alle schall fey worthe; [2]

160   They aren so ferse and so fresche, thay feghtyn bot seldom.

        I wote wele for wynnynge thay wentten fro home;   *know*

        His purse weghethe full wele that wanne thaym all hedire. [3]

        The fourte banere one the bent was brayde appon lofte,   *unfurled*

        With bothe the brerdes of blake, a balle in the myddes,   *borders*

165   Reghte siche as the sone es in someris tyde,

        When it hase moste of the mayne one Missomer Even.   *strength; Midsummer*

        That was Domynyke this daye with dynttis to dele;

        With many a blesenande beryn his banere es stuffede.   *bright; crowded*

        And sythen the pope es so priste thies prechours to helpe,   *since; willing*

170   And Frounceys with his folke es forced besyde,   *also made strong*

        And alle the ledis of the lande ledith thurgh witt,

        There es no man appon molde to machen thaym agayne,   *earth*

        Ne gete no grace appon grounde, undir God hymselven.   *anywhere*

        And yitt es the fyfte appon the felde the faireste of tham alle,

175   A brighte banere of blee whitte with three bore-hedis;

        Be any crafte that I kan Carmes thaym semyde,   *know Carmelites*

        For thay are the ordire that loven oure Lady to serve.

        If I scholde say the sothe, it semys no nothire

---

[1] *Lines 54–55: I hold that person to be a fool who would go to war even though legal disputations in court might settle the issue, / When he has found [Wynnere's] friend (the lawyer), who never failed him (in court)*

[2] *These are Saint Francis' folk, who say all are doomed to die*

[3] *He had a heavy purse who got them all to come here*

Bot that the freris with othere folke shall the felde wynn.

180	The sexte es of sendell, and so are thay alle,	*silk*
Whitte als the whalles bone, whoso the sothe tellys,	
With beltys of blake bocled togedir,	
The poyntes pared off rownde, the pendant awaye, [1]	
And alle the lethire appon lofte that one lowe hengeth	*hangs down*
185	Schynethe alle for scharpynynge of the schavynge iren:	*razor*
The ordire of the Austyns, for oughte that I wene,	*know*
For by the blussche of the belte the banere I knewe.	*gleam*
And othere synes I seghe sett appon lofte,	
Some wittnesse of wolle, and some of wyne tounnes,	*depict; casks*
190	Some of merchandes merke, so many and so thikke	*trademarks*
That I ne wote in my witt for alle this werlde riche	
Whatt segge under the sonne can the sowme rekken.	*man; sum*
And sekere one that other syde are sadde men of armes,	*certainly; sober*
Bolde sqwyeres of blode, bowmen many,	
195	That if thay strike one stroke stynt thay ne thynken	
Till owthir here appon hethe be hewen to dethe.	*either army; heath*

Forthi I bid yow bothe that thaym hedir broghte	*Therefore*
That ye wend with me, are any wrake falle,	*go; before; mischief*
To oure comely kyng that this kythe owethe;	*country possesses*
200	And fro he wiete wittirly where the wronge ristyth, [2]	
Thare nowthir wye be wrothe to wirche als he demeth." [3]	
Off ayther rowte ther rode owte a renke als me thoghte,	*man*
Knyghtis full comly one coursers attyred,	
And sayden, "Sir sandisman, sele the betyde!	*messenger, prosperity befall you*
205	Wele knowe we the kyng; he clothes us bothe,	
And hase us fosterde and fedde this fyve and twenty wyntere.	
Now fare thou byfore and we schall folowe aftire."	

---

[1] *The ends of belts (that hang down after they have passed through the buckles) are tapered to round tips, the end of the belt (tucked) away*

[2] *And from the time when he discovers for certain where the fault rests*

[3] *Let neither man be angry to act as he (the king) deems (or, let neither man be angry to act as he purposes)*

And now are thaire brydells upbrayde and bown one thaire wayes.[1]

Thay lighten doun at the launde and leved thaire stedis,   *glade*

210 Kayren up at the clyffe and one knees fallyn.   *Go*

The kynge henttis by the handes and hetys tham to ryse,   *seizes [them]; orders*

And sayde, "Welcomes, heres, as hyne of oure house bothen."[2]

The kynge waytted one wyde, and the wyne askes;   *looked*

Beryns broghte it anone in bolles of silvere.

215 Me thoghte I sowpped so sadly it sowrede bothe myn eghne.[3]

And he that wilnes of this werke to wete any forthire,   *desires; know*

Full freschely and faste, for here a fitt endes.   *Fill up*

[Fitt II]

Bot than kerpede the kynge, sayd, "Kythe what ye hatten,[4]

And whi the hates aren so hote youre hertis bytwene.   *hatreds*

220 If I schall deme yow this day, dothe me to here."   *judge; let*

"Now certys, lorde," sayde that one, "the sothe for to telle,

I hatt Wynnere, a wy that alle this werlde helpis,   *I'm called*

For I lordes cane lere thurgh ledyng of witt.   *teach*

Thoo that spedfully will spare and spende not to grete,[5]

225 Lyve appon littill-whattes, I lufe hym the bettir.   *small amounts*

Witt wiendes me with, and wysses me faire;   *goes; guides*

Aye when gadir my gudes than glades myn hert.   *my goods accumulate*

Bot this felle false thefe that byfore yowe standes   *wicked*

Thynkes to strike or he styntt and stroye me for ever.   *before*

230 Alle that I wynn thurgh witt he wastes thurgh pryde;

I gedir, I glene, and he lattys goo sone;   *immediately*

I pryke and I pryne, and he the purse opynes.   *pin; stitch together*

Why hase this cayteffe no care how men corne sellen?   *wretch*

His londes liggen alle ley, his lomes aren solde,   *lie; untilled; tools (looms)*

235 Downn bene his dowfehowses, drye bene his poles;   *dovecotes; fish pools*

---

[1] *And now are their bridles ready, and they have set out upon their ways*

[2] *"You are welcome, lords, both of you, as retainers of our house"*

[3] *It seemed I drank so deeply it bleared both my eyes*

[4] *But then the king spoke, saying, "Make known what you're named*

[5] *Those who profitably will save and spend not too much*

The devyll wounder one the wele he weldys at home,[1]

Bot hungere and heghe howses and howndes full kene.   *Nothing but*

Safe a sparthe and a spere sparrede in ane hyrne,   *battle ax; shut up; corner*

A bronde at his bede-hede, biddes he no nother   *sword*

240   Bot a cuttede capill to cayre with to his frendes.   *gelding; ride*

Then will he boste with his brande and braundesche hym ofte,   *boast; strut*

This wikkede weryed thefe that Wastoure men calles,   *accursed thief*

That if he life may longe this lande will he stroye.

Forthi deme us this daye for Drightyns love in heven[2]

245   To fighte furthe with oure folke to owthire fey worthe."   *until either dies*

"Yee, Wynnere," quod Wastoure, "thi wordes are hye: *arrogant*

Bot I schall tell the a tale that tene schall the better.   *you; vex*

When thou haste waltered and went and wakede alle the nyghte,   *tossed; turned*

And iche a wy in this werlde that wonnes the abowte,   *lives with you*

250   And hase werpede thy wyde howses full of wolle sakkes —   *filled*

The bemys benden at the rofe, siche bakone there hynges,   *bacon; hangs*

Stuffed are sterlynges undere stelen bowndes —   *silver pennies; bands*

What scholde worthe of that wele if no waste come?   *become*

Some rote, some ruste, some ratons fede.   *rats*

255   Let be thy cramynge of thi kystes for Cristis lufe of heven!   *chests*

Late the peple and the pore hafe parte of thi silvere;

For if thou wydwhare scholde walke and waytten the sothe,   *far and wide*

Thou scholdeste reme for rewthe, in siche ryfe bene the pore.   *weep; numbers*

For and thou lengare thus lyfe, leve thou no nother,   *if*

260   Thou schall be hanged in helle for that thou here spareste;   *hoard*

For siche a synn haste thou solde thi soule into helle,

And there es ever wellande woo, worlde withowtten ende."   *boiling*

"Late be thi worde, Wastoure," quod Wynnere the riche;

"Thou melleste of a mater, thou madiste it thiselven.   *complain; caused*

265   With thi sturte and thi stryffe thou stroyeste up my gudes[3]

In playinge and in wakynge in wynttres nyghttis,

In owttrage, in unthrifte, in angarte pryde.   *excess; extravagance; arrogant*

---

[1] *The devil may wonder at the wealth he enjoys at home*

[2] *Therefore judge (doom) us this day, for God's love in heaven*

[3] *With your violent behavior and contentiousness you consume my goods*

	There es no wele in this werlde to wasschen thyn handes	*well (wealth)*
	That ne es gyffen and grounden are thou it getyn have.	*spent; bestowed before*
270	Thou ledis renkes in thy rowte wele rychely attyrede;	
	Some hafe girdills of golde that more gude coste	
	Than alle the faire fre londe that ye byfore haden.	*unrestricted*
	Ye folowe noghte youre fadirs that fosterde yow alle	
	A kynde herveste to cache and cornes to wynn	
275	For the colde wyntter and the kene with gleterand frostes,	*bitter*
	Sythen dropeles drye in the dede monethe.	*After rainless drought; (March)*
	And thou wolle to the taverne, byfore the tonne-hede,	*spigot (see note)*
	Iche beryne redy with a bolle to blerren thyn eghne,	*bowl; blear*
	Hete the whatte thou have schalte and whatt thyn hert lykes,	*Order*
280	Wyfe, wedowe, or wenche that wonnes there aboute.	*dwells*
	Then es there bott "fille in" and "feche forthe," florence to schewe, [1]	
	"Wee hee," and "worthe up," wordes ynewe.	*get up; enough (many)*
	Bot when this wele es awaye, the wyne moste be payede fore;	
	Than lympis yowe weddis to laye or youre londe selle.	*it befalls; pledges*
285	For siche wikked werkes wery the oure Lorde!	*may our Lord curse you*
	And forthi God laughte that he lovede and levede that other,	*took the one*
	Iche freke one felde ogh the ferdere be to wirche. [2]	
	Teche thy men for to tille and tynen thyn feldes;	*cultivate; fence in*
	Rayse up thi rent-howses, ryme up thi yerdes,	*clear; enclosed lands*
290	Owthere hafe as thou haste done and hope aftir werse —	*what you've earned*
	That es firste the faylynge of fode, and than the fire aftir,	
	To brene the alle at a birre for thi bale dedis.	*in an instant; wicked*
	The more colde es to come, als me a clerke tolde."	
	"Yee, Wynnere," quod Wastoure, "thi wordes are vayne.	
295	With oure festes and oure fare we feden the pore;	
	It es plesynge to the Prynce that Paradyse wroghte.	
	When Cristes peple hath parte Hym payes alle the better	*it pleases Him*
	Then here ben hodirde and hidde and happede in cofers, [3]	
	That it no sonn may see thurgh seven wyntter ones,	*So that; once*
300	Owthir freres it feche when thou fey worthes,	*friars; when you die*

---

[1] *Then there's nothing but "fill the cup" and "fetch it forth," to make you show your money*

[2] *Every laborer in the field ought to be the more inspired by fear to work*

[3] *Than if goods be covered up, hidden, or laid away in chests here*

To payntten with thaire pelers or pergett with thaire walles. *pillars; plaster*
Thi sone and thi sektours, ichone slees othere;[1]
Maken dale aftir thi daye, for thou durste never. *Give a donation to the Church*
Mawngery ne myndale ne never myrthe lovediste. *Feast; memorial drink*
305 A dale aftir thi daye dose the no mare *bequest; death*
Than a lighte lanterne late appone nyghte
When it es borne at thi bakke, beryn, be my trouthe. *carried behind you*
Now wolde God that it were als I wisse couthe, *as I could devise*
That thou, Wynnere, thou wriche, and Wanhope thi brothir, *wretch; Despair*
310 And eke ymbryne dayes, and evenes of sayntes, *ember (i.e., fast; see note)*
The Frydaye and his fere one the ferrere syde, *companion (i.e., Saturday)*
Were drownede in the depe see there never droghte come,
And dedly synn for thayre dede were enditye with twelve,[2]
And thies beryns one the bynches with howes one lofte, *judges' caps*
315 That bene knowen and kydde for clerkes of the beste, *recognized*
Als gude als Arestotle or Austyn the wyse,
That alle schent were those schalkes and Scharshull itwiste,[3]
That saide I prikkede with powere his pese to distourbe! *rode out; peace*
Forthi, comely kynge, that oure case heris,
320 Late us swythe with oure swerdes swyngen togedirs; *quickly*
For nowe I se it es full sothe that sayde es full yore —
The richere of ranke wele, the rathere will drede: *in wealth; quicker*
The more havende that he hathe, the more of hert feble." *possessions*

Bot than this wrechede Wynnere full wrothely he lukes, *angrily*
325 Sayse, "this es spedles speche to speken thies wordes. *unprofitable*
Loo! this wrechide Wastoure, that wydewhare es knawenn, *far and wide*
Ne es nothir kaysser, ne kynge, ne knyghte that the folowes,
Barone, ne bachelere, ne beryn that thou loveste, *knight (in another's service)*
Bot foure felawes or fyve, that the fayth owthe; *owe you allegiance*
330 And he schall dighte thaym to dyne with dayntethes so many *summon*
That iche a wy in this werlde may wepyn for sorowe.
The bores-hede schall be broghte with plontes appon lofte, *vegetables*
Buk-tayles full brode in brothes there besyde, *bucks' hindquarters*

---

[1] *Your son and your executors, each one ruins the other*

[2] *And mortal sin, for their deaths, were indicted by a jury of twelve*

[3] *That utterly disgraced were those men and Chief Justice Shareshull together with them*

	Venyson with the frumentee, and fesanttes full riche,	*(see note)*
335	Baken mete therby one the burde sett,	*Roasted pies; table*
	Chewettes of choppede flesche, charbiande fewlis,	*Meat pies; roast fowls*
	And iche a segge that I see has sexe mens doke.	*each person; portion*
	If this were nedles note, anothir comes aftir,[1]	
	Roste with the riche sewes and the ryalle spyces,	*sauces*
340	Kiddes cloven by the rigge, quarterd swannes,	*back*
	Tartes of ten ynche, that tenys myn hert	*vexes; heart*
	To see the borde overbrade with blasande disches,	*covered; splendid*
	Als it were a rayled rode with rynges and stones.	*jewelled cross*
	The thirde mese to me were mervelle to rekken —	*course; describe*
345	For alle es Martynmesse mete that I with most dele,	*(see note)*
	Noghte bot worttes with the flesche, withowt wilde fowle	*vegetables*
	Save ane hene to hym that the howse owethe —	*(i.e., Wynnere)*
	And he will hafe birdes bownn one a broche riche,	*prepared; spit*
	Barnakes and buturs and many billed snyppes,	*geese; bitterns; snipes*
350	Larkes and lyngwhittes lapped in sogoure,	*linnets; syrup*
	Wodcokkes and wodwales full wellande hote,	*woodpeckers; boiling*
	Teeles and titmoyses to take what him lykes;	*Teals; titmice*
	[Caudel]s of conynges and custadis swete,	*Rabbit stews; open pies*
	[Dario]ls and dische-metis that ful dere coste,	*Pastries*
355	[Maw]mene that men stepen your mawes to fill,[2]	
	[Ich]e a mese at a merke bytwen twa men,[3]	
	[That s]othe bot brynneth for bale your bowells within.	*surely; burns; pain*
	[Me t]enyth at your trompers, thay tounen so heghe	*I am vexed; sound*
	[That ic]he a gome in the gate goullyng may here:[4]	
360	Then wil thay say to thamselfe, as thay samen ryden,	*together*
	Ye hafe no myster of the helpe of the heven kyng.	*need*
	Thus are ye scorned by skyll, and schathed theraftir,[5]	
	That rechen for a repaste a rawnsom of silver.	*pay; feast*
	Bot ones I herd in a haule of a herdmans tong:	*servant's*

---

[1] *As if this were not enough, another course comes after*

[2] *Mawmene (a chopped meat dish) that men steep (in wine) to fill their gullets (see note)*

[3] *Every course costs a mark for every two people*

[4] *That each man in the street may hear blaring of trumpets*

[5] *Thus are you scorned with good reason, and disgraced accordingly*

365	"Better were meles many than a mery nyghte."[1]	
	And he that wilnes of this werke for to wete forthe,	*desire; know further*
	Full freschely and faste, for here a fit endes.	*Fill up*

[Fitt III]

	"Yee, Wynnere," quod Wastour, "I wote well myselven	
	What sall lympe of the, lede, within fewe yeris.	*become*
370	Thurgh the poure plenté of corne that the peple sowes,	*absolute plenty*
	That God will graunte of his grace to growe on the erthe,	*That which*
	Ay to appaire the pris, and it passe nott to hye,	*reduce*
	Schal make the to waxe wod for wanhope in erthe,	*mad; despair*
	To hope aftir an harde yere to honge thiselven.	
375	Woldeste thou hafe lordis to lyfe as laddes on fote?	
	Prelates als prestes that the parischen yemes?	*look after*
	Prowde marchandes of pris as pedders in towne?	*wealth; peddlers*
	Late lordes lyfe als tham liste, laddes as tham falles;	*Let; please*
	Thay the bacon and beefe, thay botours and swannes,	*Let these have; bitterns*
380	Thay the roughe of the rye, thay the rede whete,	*husk; fine*
	Thay the grewell gray, and thay the gude sewes;	*gruel; sauces*
	And then may the peple hafe parte in povert that standes,	
	Sum gud morsell of mete to mend with thair chere.	*improve their condition*
	If fewlis flye schold forthe and fongen be never,	*caught*
385	And wild bestis in the wodde wone al thaire lyve,	
	And fisches flete in the flode, and ichone ete other,	*swim; eat each other*
	Ane henne at ane halpeny by halfe yeris ende,[2]	
	Schold not a ladde be in londe a lorde for to serve.	
	This wate thou full wele witterly thiselven,	*certainly*
390	Whoso wele schal wyn, a wastour moste he fynde,	*Whoever wealth*
	For if it greves one gome, it gladdes another."	*man*
	"Now," quod Wynner to Wastour, "me wondirs in hert	
	Of thies poure penyles men that peloure will by,	*fur*
	Sadills of sendale, with sercles full riche.	*costly fabric; rings*
395	Lesse and ye wrethe your wifes, thaire willes to folowe,	*Lest you anger*

---

[1] *"Regular meals would be better than a single merry feast"*

[2] *A hen would cost a halfpenny by the end of half a year*

	Ye sellyn wodd aftir wodde in a wale tyme,	*quickly*
	Bothe the oke and the assche and all that ther growes;	
	The spyres and the yonge sprynge ye spare to your children,	*shoots; sapling*
	And sayne God wil graunt it his grace to grow at the last,	
400	For to save to your sones: bot the schame es your ownn.	
	Nedeles save ye the soyle, for sell it ye thynken.	
	Your forfadirs were fayne, when any frende come,	*glad*
	For to schake to the schawe and schewe hym the estres,[1]	
	In iche holt that thay had ane hare for to fynde,	
405	Bryng to the brod lande bukkes ynewe	*enough*
	To lache and to late goo, to lightten thaire hertis.	*catch*
	Now es it sett and solde, my sorowe es the more,	*leased*
	Wastes alle wilfully, your wyfes to paye.	*please*
	That are had lordes in londe and ladyes riche,	*Those who once*
410	Now are thay nysottes of the new gett, so nysely attyred,[2]	
	With side slabbande sleves, sleght to the grounde,	*ample drooping; let down*
	Ourlede all umbtourne with ermyn aboute,	*Trimmed; around*
	That es as harde, as I hope, to handil in the derne,	*dark*
	Als a cely symple wenche that never silke wroghte.	*innocent; worked with*
415	Bot whoso lukes on hir lyre, oure Lady of Heven,	*misfortune*
	How scho fled for ferd ferre out of hir kythe,	*fear far*
	Appon ane amblande asse, withowtten more pride,	
	Safe a barne in hir barme, and a broken heltre	*child; lap; halter*
	That Joseph held in hys hande, that hend for to yeme,	*gracious one; guard*
420	Allthofe scho walt al this werlde, hir wedes wer pore	*ruled; clothes*
	For to gyf ensample of siche, for to schewe other	
	For to leve pompe and pride, that poverté ofte schewes."[3]	
	Than the Wastour wrothly castes up his eghne,	
	And said, "Thou Wynnere, thou wriche, me wondirs in hert	
425	What hafe oure clothes coste the, caytef, to by,	*villain; buy*
	That thou schal birdes upbrayd of thair bright wedis,	*ladies; clothes*
	Sythen that we vouchesafe that the silver payen.	
	It lyes wele for a lede his leman to fynde,	*loved one; provide for*

---

[1] *To go into the woods to show him the recesses of the estate*

[2] *Now they (the wives) are foolish girls of the new fashion, so foolishly dressed*

[3] *Lines 421–22: In order to give such an example, to show others / That they should leave pomp and pride, (something) which poverty often teaches.*

Aftir hir faire chere to forthir hir herte.

430 Then will scho love hym lelely as hir lyfe one, *loyally*

Make hym bolde and bown with brandes to smytte, *ready*

To schonn schenchipe and schame ther schalkes ere gadird; [1]

And if my peple ben prode, me payes alle the better [2]

To see tham faire and free tofore with myn eghne. *lavish; in my presence*

435 And ye negardes appon nyghte ye nappen so harde, *misers; sleep; soundly*

Routten at your raxillyng, raysen your hurdes; *Snore as you stretch; buttocks*

Ye beden wayte one the wedir, then wery ye the while [3]

That ye nade hightilde up your houses and your hyne raysed. [4]

Forthi, Wynnere, with wronge thou wastes thi tyme;

440 For gode day ne glade getys thou never.

The devyll at thi dede-day schal delyn thi gudis; *distribute*

Tho thou woldest that it were, wyn thay it never; *Those*

Thi skathill sectours schal sever tham aboute, *wicked executors*

And thou hafe helle full hotte for that thou here saved.

445 Thou tast tent one a tale that tolde was full yore: *take heed of*

I hold hym madde that mournes his make for to wyn [5]

Hent hir that hir haf schal, and hold hir his while, *Let him take*

Take the coppe as it comes, the case as it falles,

For whoso lyfe may lengeste lympes to feche *gets to fetch*

450 Woodd that he waste schall to warmen his helys, *heels*

Ferrere than his fadir dide by fyvetene myle. *Farther*

Now kan I carpe no more; bot, Sir Kyng, by thi trouthe, *speak*

Deme us where we duell schall: me thynke the day hyes. *Decree; flies*

Yit harde sore es myn hert and harmes me more

455 Ever to see in my syghte that I in soule hate." *the one that I*

The kynge lovely lokes on the ledis twayne,

Says, "Blynnes, beryns, of youre brethe and of youre brode worde, *Cease*

And I schal deme yow this day where ye duelle schall, *inform*

Aythere lede in a lond ther he es loved moste. *Either person*

---

[1] *To avoid ignominy and shame where men are gathered*

[2] *And if my people are proudly arrayed, I am pleased all the better*

[3] *You give orders to wait on the weather, then curse the time*

[4] *That you had not prepared your houses and organized your servants*

[5] *I hold that person crazy who worries about winning his mate*

460	Wende, Wynnere, thi waye over the wale stremys,	*Go; swift/pleasant*
	Passe forthe by Paris to the Pope of Rome;	
	The cardynalls ken the wele, will kepe the ful faire,	*know you well*
	And make thi sydes in silken schetys to lygge,	
	And fede the and foster the and forthir thyn hert,	
465	As leefe to worthen wode as the to wrethe ones. [1]	
	Bot loke, lede, be thi lyfe, when I lettres sende,	*by your life*
	That thou hy the to me home on horse or one fote;	*hasten*
	And when I knowe thou will co[me], he schall cayre uttire,	*go further away*
	And lenge with another lede, til thou thi lefe [take];	*stay; leave*
470	For thofe thou bide in this burgh to thi be[ryinge-daye],	*remain; death*
	With hym happyns the never a fote for [to holde]. [2]	
	And thou, Wastoure, I will that thou wonn[e scholde]	*should dwell*
	Ther moste waste es of wele, and wyng [ther until].	*Where; hurry thither*
	Chese the forthe into the Chepe, a chambre thou rere, [3]	
475	Loke thi wyndowe be wyde, and wayte the aboute,	*See to it; watch*
	Where any potet beryn thurgh the burgh passe;	*drunk*
	Teche hym to the taverne till he tayte worthe;	*becomes merry*
	Doo hym drynk al nyghte that he dry be at morow,	*Make him*
	Sythen ken hym to the crete to comforth his vaynes,	*show; Cretan wine*
480	Brynge hym to Bred Strete, bikken thi fynger, [4]	
	Schew hym of fatt chepe scholdirs ynewe,	*sheep*
	"Hotte for the hungry," a hen other twayne,	
	Sett hym softe one a sege, and sythen send after,	*seat; send for supplies*
	Bryng out of the burgh the best thou may fynde,	
485	And luke thi knave hafe a knoke bot he the clothe sprede.	*beating unless*
	Bot late hym paye or he passe, and pik hym so clene	*before; rob*
	That fynd a peny in his purse and put owte his eghe. [5]	
	When that es dronken and don, duell ther no lenger,	
	Bot teche hym owt of the townn to trotte aftir more.	*show*
490	Then passe to the Pultrie, the peple the knowes,	*Poultry (in Cheapside)*
	And ken wele thi katour to knawen thi fode,	*instruct; buyer*

---

[1] *As willing to go mad as to anger you (even) once*

[2] *I.e., no matter how long Winner remains in the land, he will not be able to keep up with Waster*

[3] *Go forth into Cheapside, a chamber set up there*

[4] *Bring him to Bread Streat (in Cheapside, noted for its bakeries), beckon with your finger*

[5] *That if anyone find a penny in his purse, let him be damned (have his eyes put out)*

The herons, the hasteletez, the henne wele serve,   *roast meats*

The pertrikes, the plovers, the other pulled byrddes, *partridges; plucked*

The albus, this other foules, the egretes dere; *bullfinches; white herons*

495 The more thou wastis thi wele, the better the Wynner lykes. *spend*

And wayte to me, thou Wynnere, if thou wilt wele chefe, *look; prosper*

When I wende appon werre my wyes to lede; *war*

For at the proude pales of Parys the riche *palace*

I thynk to do it in ded, and dub the to knyghte,

500 And giff giftes full grete of golde and of silver,

To ledis of my legyance that lufen me in hert.

And sythen kayre as I come, with knyghtes that me foloen,

To the kirk of Colayne ther the kynges ligges. . . . *cathedral*

Explanatory Notes

T refers to Trigg's edition of the poem; T-P to Turville-Petre's 1989 edition; G to Gollancz's edition.

1–2   A number of alliterative poems (most famously *Sir Gawain and the Green Knight*) open by referring to Britain's founding by Brutus, the great-grandson of Aeneas. The legend stems from Geoffrey of Monmouth's *Historia Regum Britanniae*. The tradition of Aeneas' treason in betraying Troy was also well known in the Middle Ages; it stems from Servius' commentary on the *Aeneid*. For a poem that probably alludes to the Statute of Treasons (see below, note to 130ff.), the opening seems particularly apt.

4   *nyne.* Cardinals in Middle English are used for ordinals fairly frequently (Tauno F. Mustanoja, *A Middle English Syntax, I: Parts of Speech. Mémoires de la Société Néophilologique de Helsinki* 23 [1960], p. 306). On the chaos of the time Turville-Petre (1989) observes: "The brilliant victories over the French at Crécy and Calais in 1346–47 were succeeded in 1348 and the following years by the horrors of the Black Death, when it seemed that, with starvation, increased crime and a severe shortage of labour, economic and moral order was collapsing" (p. 41).

5   *witt and wyles.* The poet alludes to abuse of two of man's three faculties, *intellect* and *will*. *Memory* is the third.

10–16   Political prophecies of this sort were not uncommon in England during the later Middle Ages: Thomas of Erceldoune's *Prophecy* (4–5), for instance, parallels the impossible situation of finding hares on hearthstones. These prophecies, as indeed the entire genre of complaint they are part of, emerge from an old tradition in which the "abuses of the age" are catalogued (Bestul, pp. 55–58). The effect of such pronouncements did not pass unnoticed: in 1402 a law was passed which forbade the making of prophecies. Invoking the Apocalypse and Judgment Day in particular was common in French and English allegorical romances of the time. Solomon's reputation in the Middle Ages as not only a sage but magician and prophet makes him a fitting figure to evoke, especially in a debate poem.

15   *lede hem at will*. T-P and G read: *lede at hir will*. But T notes that *leden*, "marry," normally requires a direct object (p. 18).

19–23   Criticism of present-day poets and jongleurs was familiar in medieval allegories and histories. Perhaps closest to *Wynnere* is the Chandos Herald, who in the Prologue to his *Life and Deeds of the Black Prince* (lines 1–30), written in French, says that "once those who made fine poems were regarded as men of authority, but now greater heed is paid to a chatterer, a false liar, a juggler, or a jester."

21   *in fere*. The reference to companions here perhaps alludes to patronage.

24   *chyn-wedys*. T-P points to the derisive mockery of the word, which is modeled on heroic vocabulary (e.g., *here-wedys*, "battle-garments," i.e., armor).

25   *thies*. T-P and G emend to *three*.

32   Wandering in the west beside a stream is a common convention in Middle English poetry; see Bestul, p. 66.

36   *hill*. "Hill" could possibly mean a mound overgrown with plants here, as it does in *Pearl*, line 41 (Elliott).

       hawthorne. The hawthorn tree was sometimes associated with the supernatural world (T). Compare *Death and Liffe* (lines 30–31) and *The Romance of the Rose* (line 4002), where the hawthorn also appears (T-P).

39   *Bernacles*. Barnacle geese were exotic creatures: they were thought to grow in shells which adhered to trees overhanging water (T).

40   *foles*. T-P: *fowles*.

50   The armies of Wynnere and Wastoure are in either woods, separated by the glade.

58   *appon hate*. This is the MS reading; T, T-P, and G emend to *hethe*. For "upon" as "in," see line 67: *appon Ynglisse tonge*, and *OED sv.* 10b. As in the Middle

English *The Wars of Alexander* (line 42), "upon" here denotes a state or condition; it was often associated with states of hostility. There is no need to emend the MS.

59–68   Following Speirs, Elliott argues that the topography of the dream recalls settings used in the medieval circular theater, as well as the lists of medieval tournaments and pageantry. The *caban* here, for instance, corresponds to the highly decorated judge's box or pavilion at fourteenth-century English tournaments. Although the cabin is adorned with emblems of the Order of the Garter (see note to line 68), one should observe that Edward III's tournaments consisted of series of single combats, not the mock battles of an earlier age. Juliet Vale (pp. 73–75) suggests that a scene like the one described in the poem may have been part of the Christmas "ludi," or court games, that were held in 1352: in them there appeared a group dressed as Dominicans and another dressed as merchants, both with their own banners.

64   *ther.* MS: *thre.* T: *th[er]*; T-P: *the*; G: *th[ies].* *he.* T: *he[u].*

66   *fresche.* T-P: *Frensche.*

68   This line translates *"Honi soit qui mal y pense,"* the motto of the Order of the Garter, which was formed by Edward III in either 1347 or 48; it was apparently officially instituted in 1349. The Order consisted of the king and twenty-six chosen knights, each of whom wore a blue garter circumscribed with gold (see line 62), which symbolized a lasting bond of friendship and honor. Edward also had a round table made for his knights.

70   *holt.* T-P: *hale.*

71   *wodwyse.* The wildman was a popular figure of untamed strength in medieval pageantry, art, heraldry, and literature (T). For a brief account, see Larry Benson, *Art and Tradition in Sir Gawain and the Green Knight* (New Brunswick: Rutgers University Press, 1965), pp. 72–83; the standard study is Richard Bernheimer, *Wild Men in the Middle Ages* (Cambridge, Mass.: Harvard University Press, 1952). Some of Edward III's own livery seems to have been decorated with *"wode woses"* (T-P: 45). "Dressing up" had become common in tournaments by the end of the fourteenth century (Glynne Wickham, *Early English Stages 1300–1600,* [New York: Columbia University Press, 1980], I, 42–44); the "wild man" was one of the figures people dressed up as.

76–82   The "wodwyse" bears the royal arms of England on his lambrequin, a mantle that hangs from the back of his helmet.

78–80   The heraldry of Edward, the Black Prince, bears the fleur-de-lis of France in the top left and bottom right quarters of the field *(before and behynde)* and the three rampant leopards (heraldically called lions) of England on the upper right *(one lofte)* and lower left *(on lowe undir)*. As T-P notes: "The arms of France were quartered with those of England in 1340 with reference to Edward III's claims to the French Throne" (p. 45).

79   *with sex grim bestes*, as in MS. T: *with [orfraied] bestes;* T-P: *with sex egre bestes;* G: *with sex [irous] bestes.*

83   *knyghte*: MS: *kynge.* The emendation, accepted by most editors, avoids referring to the king, who is inside the pavilion, not next to it, before the narrator actually sees him three lines later. T-P, however, retains the MS reading and interprets the line: "by the (heraldry of) the pavilion I recognized the King that I was looking at" (p. 45). In his 1982 edition T-P identified the king specifically as Edward III.

90–92   These lines are difficult. I have followed Turville-Petre in retaining the MS reading and see *Bery-brown was his berde* as an awkward ellipsis that refers to Edward, whose beard was in fact brown. Gollancz emends *was* to *as*, and interprets the king's clothes to be the same color as his beard. Trigg, however, may be right to say that these lines are among the most corrupt in the poem; her emendation is *Bery broun was [the bleaunt]*, i.e., the material.

94   *gerede full riche.* The MS reads: *girde in the myddes,* which the scribe probably anticipated from the following line. If the MS reading is retained, as in T-P, the sense would be that the garters were wrapped around the middle of the birds.

97   *daderande tham semede.* A dative form could have a nominative function with an impersonal verb in Middle English. "Seem" was in transition from an impersonal to a personal verb at the time (Mustanoja, *A Middle English Syntax*, pp. 112–13).

100   Edward was known for his love of hawking.

115ff   Various attempts have been made to identify the herald from his jupon: Gollancz suggested the Black Prince, Salter a member of the Wingfield family. Sir John Wingfield was chief administrator for the Black Prince from 1351–61. As Trigg notes, however, wings were a common heraldic device.

Reed, *Middle English Debate Poetry* (pp. 264–66), suggests that in sending a minister to pray for peace and to summon feuding parties to appear before the king for arbitration of their dispute, the poet recalls the protocols of Parliament, which also opened with a call for peace and the king's declaration that he is willing to decide the pleas of his people.

121   *caughte.* MS reads *caughten,* which is ungrammatical. Editors who emend for reasons of alliteration suggest: T-P *broched in* ("urged his horse in swiftly"); G *brawndeschet* ("brandished"); T *brayede* ("seized").

125   *Send his.* The MS form is kept here as a possible contraction of *sendeth.* T and G emend to *Sendes.* Gollancz's emendation of *erande* to *bodword* is tempting.

127   *no.* Again the MS reading is kept. For *no* = "nor," see *MED, s.v., conj.*

130ff   These lines have been thought to refer to the Statute of Treasons of 1352. Salter has shown that if this is the case, the poet's allusion is at best very general, for the offenses in the poem, abrogation of the king's privilege to ride with unfurled banners and disturbing his peace, correspond imprecisely with the stipulations of the Statute, which in fact classified the act of leading one armed band against another as a felony rather than as a treasonable offense. On the other hand, by using the word *ryall* (line 128), the messenger seems to imply that the armies have committed a treasonable offense, and riding with banners displayed was, as T-P notes (p. 45), evidence of levying open war, which remained an act of treason under international law.

Furthermore, as Trigg notes, the phrase *"his pese to disturbe,"* both here and at line 318, might deliberately echo William Shareshull (see note to line 317), who summoned Parliament to draft the Statute of Treasons by saying that "the King has understood that the peace of his realm has not been kept as it should have been, and that the disturbers of the peace and maintainers of quarrels and riots in the land have harmed many of its people." Even though this phrasing is formulaic, it does seem likely, all told, that the poet is making some reference to the Statute here.

136   *amonges thies wyes one.* The MS reading is retained despite the diffuseness of
        syntax and possible error of repeating *one* from the line preceding. T and G
        emend to *thies wyes amonges.*

144   *bulles.* The MS reading is *bibulles,* which could possibly mean "Bibles," though
        the orthography is against it. T, G, and T-P all emend to *bulles.* Holinshed
        (*Chronicles*) reports that in 1343 one challenger in a tournament held at
        Smithfield came dressed as the pope, and brought twelve others with him who
        were dressed as cardinals (Bestul, p. 103). During the 1340s and 50s, feelings
        in England ran high against the Pope, whose power and demands for money
        were conveyed by pronouncements known as bulls.

149–55 The "band of green" on the lawyers' banner has been associated with the
        "green wax" used to seal a writ. The extra cost for such sealing (sixpence),
        without which a sheriff could not receive the writ, provided income for lawyers
        and a popular target for those who satirized them.

157   *galegs.* Emended from MS *galeys* by all editors. As part of their vow of poverty,
        Franciscans were supposed to go shoeless, but wearing the simple *galegs,* a kind
        of shoe the apostles were thought to have worn, seems to have been an accept-
        ed practice among the friars.

163   *was.* T-P emends to *es.*

164   *balle.* An emendation of MS *balke,* accepted by all editors.

166   *mayne.* The MS reads *maye,* which makes little sense. All editors emend to
        mayne, which gives the line the sense "when the sun is at its strongest." Havely
        argues that the banner contains elements, such as its emphasis on light, that
        are drawn from Dominican iconography and hagiography.

176, 186 Internal details suggest that these lines have been transposed by the scribe. The
        Carmelites (known as White friars) were famous for their devotion to the
        Virgin (see line 177); the Augustinian friars wore black habits with leather
        girdles (see lines 182–87). The three boarsheads are a common heraldic sign;
        if they are indeed on the banner of the White friars, this resonates with the
        fact that Carmelites were charged in particular to be abstemious and to prac-
        tice frugality.

177 *ordire.* Most editors emend to *ledis* for reasons of alliteration. The pattern *xa/ax* is found in the poem, but, as Trigg notes, only when voiced/unvoiced or couplet alliteration is involved. Still, the poem is too short to rule out the possibility that the same pattern could occur in other circumstances: it appears three times in *Parlement.*

189–90 *Some wittnesse of wolle.* The MS has *Some of witnesse of wolle.* This entails taking *wittnesse* as a noun rather than a verb, which is possible, but awkward. For "merke" in the next line as a generic plural, "trademarks," see *MED, s.v.* 5a.

193 After the lengthy elaboration of Wynnere's army, the brevity of the description of Wastoure's forces is striking. What this terseness means, however, is open to debate.

197 *hedir broghte.* T-P: *broghte hedir.*

201 *wye.* The MS *wyes* is an error for the singular form.

    demeth. The MS reads *doeth,* which makes little sense. Most editors emend as here.

215 *sowrede.* T-P: *sowed.*

217 See note to line 367.

236 *The devyll wounder one.* More idiomatic ME usage would omit the *one,* since it seems to make *wounder* a verb when it actually is a noun.

237 *heghe howses.* These have been interpreted as houses Wastoure owns but has not rented. The phrase, however, often carried connotations of pride and ostentation: see *MED s.v.* 1a.

248 Compare *Parlement,* lines 257–60. The merchant who cannot sleep for worry about his goods is a familiar convention.

254 *Some rote, some ruste.* See Matt. 6:19–21.

256–62 See Matt. 25:31–46.

264   *thou*. The MS reads *tho,* "although"; accepting this reading, the line would mean "You speak of a matter although (you) caused it yourself." As Trigg points out, however, the conjunction is spelled *thofe* elsewhere in the poem, and *thou* nicely completes the line: Wynnere says Wastoure's excessive consumption has caused the shortages that have made so many poor. T-P and G: *thou*.

266   *playinge*. This is the MS reading; it has been variously emended on grounds of alliteration. Some suggested emendations: *wayttinge,* feasting; *wraxling(e),* *wrastlinge,* wrestling; *wastinge*. See T's note (pp. 33–34) for a summary of the proposed readings.

267   *angarte pryde*. T-P: *augarte pryde;* G: *angarte [of] pryde*.

270   *rychely*. MS: *ryhely*. All editors emend to *rychely*.

276   *dede monethe*. The drought of March was a recognized (and welcomed) feature of the climate of medieval England: see A. Stuart Daley, "Chaucer's 'droghte of March' in Medieval Farm Lore," *Chaucer Review* 4 (1970), 171–79.

277–82   Compare this tavern scene and *Piers Plowman* A.5.185 and 8.67–75.

277   *tonne-hede*. This could be read as *toune-hede,* the upper extremity of a town.

282   T-P (p. 55) points to the sexual allusions: *"Wee hee"* is the noise of an amorous horse; *worthe up:* "climb up."

286   The allusion is to Matt. 24:40.

288   *tynen*. The MS reads *tymen,* which Karen Stern (University of London M. Phil. thesis, 1973) and Lon Mark Rosenfeld (Columbia University dissertation, 1975) interpret as "tames, subdues." Most, however, accept the emendation and gloss "fence in"; Burrow glosses the sense as "harrows."

300   *freres it feche*. Friars were often named the recipients of goods in wills. See *Piers Plowman's Crede* lines 404–17, where the friar is so eager to collect upon a wealthy widow's death that he can't stay to answer Will's questions.

308ff.   Wastoure implies that Wynnere is so full of worry, he and Wanhope (despair of God's mercy) are kin. Wastoure then goes on to wish that the penances imposed by the Church were drowned in the sea. He then derisively imagines the legal charges for their "deaths," and defies the charge that he would be disturbing the peace for having gotten rid of Wynnere, Wanhope, and the others.

310   *ymbryne dayes.* Ember days: a three day period of fasting (Wednesday and the following Friday and Saturday) appointed by the Church during each of the four seasons. Fasts were decreed the day before a Saint's day as well; Fridays and Saturdays were always days of abstinence.

317   Sir William Shareshull (?1289–1370), Chief Justice from 1350–61, earned the hatred of many in all classes of society for his part in promulgating restrictive legislation of all kinds, especially the Statute of Laborers in 1351 and the Statute of Treasons in the following year. See Bertha Putnam, *The Place in Legal History of Sir William Shareshull* (Cambridge: Cambridge University Press, 1950). Both Steadman (1923) and Anderson suggest these lines refer to an uprising in Chester in 1353, where Shareshull held a general eyre (i.e., circuit court).

    itwiste. The MS reads *it wiste*; the line would mean then that Wastoure wants all those destroyed — and Shareshull knew it — who said he disturbed the peace. *Itwiste,* "together with them," however, makes better sense and is consistent with the scribe's practice of separating the elements of prepositions and pronouns (he writes *by syde* and *hym selven* for *bysyde* and *hymselven*).

329   *owthe.* The only instance of a Southern ending for the present tense (T). The form has legal implications; it suggests that Wastoure's followers have entered into sworn legal contracts with him.

332ff.   Descriptions of sumptuous feasts are common in Middle English romances: compare *Morte Arthure*, lines 176–215. The one described here follows the usual sequence of courses.

334   *frumentee.* A potage made of boiled hulled grain mixed with almond milk and sweeteners; often served with venison.

337   *doke.* This is the MS reading, though the emendation to *dole,* "portion" is very tempting. T emends to *dole.* G translates *doke* as "dole," comparing the term to *docket,* or "piece."

345   *Martynmesse.* November 11, the feast celebrating St. Martin of Tours, at butchering time when salting of meat for winter storage was taking place.

353–59   The MS has lost a small piece from the top left hand corner at this point. The emendations follow those suggested by Gollancz, Burrow (line 356), and Trigg (line 357).

355   *[Maw]mene that men stepen.* A new reading. All editors have read *clepen,* translating "what men call mawmene." The manuscript, however, almost certainly reads *stepen. Mawmene* is a chopped meat dish that very often was made with wine: see *MED, s.v.* for citations. Wynnere is describing a variation of the dish in which the meat has been soaked in wine.

356   G: *[Twelve] mese at a merke;* T-P: *Aye a mese at a merke.* T-P notes (p. 59) that in 1349 a mark (160 pence) could buy two horses.

357   T-P: *Siche bot brynneth for bale . . .;* G: *[Thog]he bot brynneth for bale. . . .*

361   *myster.* T-P emends to *hope,* noting that *"myster,* 'need', neither alliterates nor makes sense" (p. 59).

364   *ones.* MS: *one.*

366   *forthe.* T-P emends to *forthire.*

367   *Full freschely and faste.* The invitation to fill one's cup with drink for the next fitt suggests an oral presentation (see line 217). T comments on the irony of the invitation, given the account of Wastoure's feast. "The repeated lines seem to be a stylistic remnant of the minstrel's art; certainly the fitt divisions perform little formal or structural function as the poem is too short (barely longer than a single fitt of *Sir Gawain and the Green Knight*) and its action too continuous to require the pauses. The lines calling for wine are part of the poet's overall fiction, reminding us of the dreamer's presence, with the address to the readers at line 31" (p. 36).

370–74   These lines are difficult. Their sense perhaps is: "Because crops will be good, the price for them will remain low, which will drive Wynnere mad with despair (because of the reduced value of his crops, if we take *erthe*="ploughing"), and make him (either) hope for a hard year (to drive the prices back up), (or) hang

39

himself." Alternatively, lines 373–74 can mean that Wynnere will expect a hard year (for himself) to follow, which will lead him to hang himself.

372 *and it passe.* MS: *and passe.* T's emendation. T-P and G read *that it passe.*

375ff. For the argument that expenditure is necessary to maintain honor and reputation, see *The Romance of the Rose*, lines 5232–48.

384–88 These lines seem to mean that without consumption (by the rich), food would become so plentiful and cheap that the poor would have no incentive to work, and the social order would thus be threatened.

386 *ete.* T-P and G emend to *frete* ("devour"), for the sake of alliteration and ferocity.

390 *moste.* MS: *moþe,* in margin with caret marks.

392ff. Wynnere sarcastically dismisses Wastoure's contention (lines 382–83) that by his spending the lot of the poor will improve.

400 *For to save to youre sones.* This is the MS reading. It makes adequate, if redundant, sense; its grammar is awkward, but passable. Many editors follow Gollancz and emend to *schadowe,* "provide shade for."

409 T emends to *That are had [ben] lordes . . .* on the grounds that this continues Wynnere's argument against the dissolute nobility. T-P emends *had* to *were.* It is possible, though, that having spoken of those who have squandered their ancestral estate, Wynnere shows his own concern for the social hierarchy by turning to those who once were servants but now, able to command higher wages, are imitating the upper classes. The passage, nonetheless, is obscure, as is the comparison to the simple maid that ends it; it does seem to pivot, however, about the thought that clothes do not alter the nature of those who wear them.

411 *side slabbende sleves.* The MS reads *elde,* which does stand in contrast to the *new gett* of the line before, but the sense is difficult. Most editors emend to *side* "wide." Attacks on long sleeves were common in satires of the period. T-P emends to *sleȝe* ("skillfully made").

415ff.   The passage ends as it began, with the poor, but whether the humility and poverty of Mary and Joseph is an example more to be set against Wynnere or Wastoure is hard to say at this point.

422   *schewes.* G emends to *eschewes,* glossing the line to mean: "To leave pomp and pride that poverty scorn."

428ff   Compare *Parlement,* 246–60.

434   *To see tham faire and free.* The MS probably reads *To fee tham . . . ,* which would mean that Wastoure is all the happier, if his people are proudly attired, to hire them *(enfeoff)* at a generous wage; there are difficulties, however, with this reading, despite its preferability in alliteration. Though T-P reads *fee,* G and T read *see,* which makes better sense. The *f* and *s* are easily confused, especially late in the MS.

435ff.   Again it is hard to determine exactly the point of Wastoure's thrust: is he saying (as in line 248) that Wynnere can't sleep because he's worried about his goods? The MS readings, preserved here, however, suggest the opposite: that Wynnere sleeps too soundly, suggesting a slothfulness that is seconded by Wastoure's charge that Wynnere wastes time by putting off making needed repairs to his storehouses and by failing to organize his household to react to a small harvest, if the weather is bad, or a large one, if it is good (T). T-P (p. 62) suggests that Wynnere makes a virtue of his slothfulness, first instructing his men to wait and then cursing because it is too late to do anything: thus the miser saves money in repairs and labor.

445   *Thou tast tent.* T, G, and T-P emend to *Thou tast no tent.*

446   *make.* G emends to *makende* and translates the line: "I hold him mad that worries such winnings to make."

451   *Ferrere.* The implication seems to be that the person who happens to live longest has to go farther to fetch wood because the timber from the surrounding countryside for fifteen miles around has already been cut down.

454   *myn hert and harmes.* MS: *hert* omitted. All recent editors follow G's emendation. T observes: "The scribe's characteristic error of omission is easily corrected" (p. 45).

460 *wale.* Rosenfeld derives the word from OE *wael,* "dangerous, deadly." T suggests "fine, beautiful, pleasant" as perhaps more appropriate. G suggests "swift, quick, moving."

468–73 Part of the manuscript has been cut away here. I have followed Trigg's emendations.

476 *potet.* An obscure word; Turville-Petre (1982) glosses as "?tippler," a guess I have adopted, though in his 1989 edition he emends to "*botet* 'booted', i.e., 'equipped for riding'" (p. 64). The situation would somewhat recall that of the Manciple and Cook in *The Canterbury Tales.* Other suggestions include emending to *potener,* "one who carries a purse" (G); *pert* (Stern); *potent* (Rosenfeld); and *petit,* "insignificant" (T).

479 *to comforth his vaynes.* T-P compares the Cretan wine as comfort for hangover to "the hair of the dog" (p. 65).

482 *Hotte for the hungry* seems to echo a street vendor's cry. T compares the line to *Piers Plowman* A Prol.104–05 and "London Lickpenny," lines 59ff. (R. H. Robbins, *Historical Poems,* no. 51).

485 *sprede.* MS: *spre.* T-P and G: *spred;* T: *spre[de].*

494 *this other foules.* Probably, as Trigg says, a scribal substitution for an illegible or unfamiliar word. She suggests *endes,* "ducks"; others read *osulles,* "ouzels."

498 T-P (p. 65) identifies the *proude pales* as the "Palais de la Cité." He points out that after 1346, Edward was eager to press his claim to the French crown; he tempted investors and soldiers to underwrite a campaign, whose costs were very high, with the promise of rich profits that could be made.

500 *silver.* MS: *si.* All emend to *silver.*

502 *kayre.* MS: *layren.* I follow T's emendation. G and T-P: *kayren.*

503 A reference to the shrine of the Three Magi in Cologne Cathedral. Gollancz points out that Edward III visited and made offerings at the shrine in 1338.

The Parlement of the Thre Ages

	In the monethe of Maye when mirthes bene fele,	*joys are many*
	And the sesone of somere when softe bene the wedres,	*breezes*
	Als I went to the wodde my werdes to dreghe,	*to try my luck*
	Into the schawes myselfe a schotte me to gete	*thickets*
5	At ane hert or ane hynde, happen as it myghte;	*hart; hind*
	And as Dryghtyn the day drove frome the heven,	
	Als I habade one a banke be a bryme syde,	*abided; side of a stream*
	There the gryse was grene, growen with floures,	*grass*
	The primrose, the pervynke, and piliole the riche,	*periwinkle; penny-royal*
10	The dewe appon dayses donkede full faire,	*spread moisture*
	Burgons and blossoms and braunches full swete,	*Buds*
	And the mery mystes full myldely gane falle;	*did*
	The cukkowe, the cowschote, kene were thay bothen,	*wood-pigeons; lively*
	And the throstills full throly threpen in the bankes,	*vigorously contend in song*
15	And iche foule in that frythe faynere than other	*each bird; woods; more glad*
	That the derke was done and the daye lightenede.	*night*
	Hertys and hyndes one hillys thay gouen,	*stare intently (?)*
	The foxe and the filmarte thay flede to the erthe;	*polecat*
	The hare hurkles by hawes and harde thedir dryves,	*huddles; hedges*
20	And ferkes faste to hir fourme and fatills hir to sitt. [1]	
	Als I stode in that stede one stalkynge I thoghte:	*place*
	Bothe my body and my bowe I buskede with leves,	*camouflaged*
	And turnede towardes a tree and tariede there a while.	
	And als I lokede to a launde a littill me besyde,	*glade*
25	I seghe ane hert with ane hede, ane heghe for the nones: [2]	
	Alle unburneschede was the beme, full borely the mydle,	*unpolished; massive*
	With iche feetur as thi fote, forfrayed in the greves,	*tine; rubbed clean; groves*
	With auntlers one aythere syde egheliche longe.	*fearsomely*

22

---

[1] *And hastens (forks) swiftly to her den and makes herself ready to rest*

[2] *I saw a hart with a head of antlers, a large rack, indeed*

The ryalls full richely raughten frome the myddes, [1]

30 With surryals full semely appon sydes twayne; *(see note)*

And he assommet and sett of six and of fyve, [2]

And therto borely and brode and of body grete, *massive; broad*

And a coloppe for a kynge, cache hym who myghte. *tasty bit of meat*

Bot there sewet hym a sorwe that servet hym full yerne, [3] *(see note)*

35 That woke and warned hym when the wynde faylede,

That none so sleghe in his slepe with sleghte scholde hym dere, *sly; harm*

And went the wayes hym byfore when any wothe tyde. *danger befell*

My lyame than full lightly lete I doun falle, *leash*

And to the bole of a birche my berselett I cowchide; [4]

40 I waitted wiesly the wynde by waggynge of leves, *judged shrewdly*

Stalkede full stilly no stikkes to breke,

And crepite to a crabtre and coverede me therundere.

Then I bende up my bowe and bownede me to schote, *strung; prepared*

Tighte up my tylere and taysede at the hert. [5]

45 Bot the sowre that hym sewet sett up the nese, *soar; followed; nose*

And wayttede wittyly abowte and wyndide full yerne. [6]

Then I moste stonde als I stode and stirre no fote ferrere, *further*

For had I myntid or movede or made any synys, *taken aim; signs*

Alle my layke hade bene loste that I hade longe wayttede. *sport*

50 Bot gnattes gretely me grevede and gnewen myn eghne; *bit; eyes*

And he stotayde and stelkett and starede full brode, [7]

Bot at the laste he loutted doun and laughte till his mete, *bent; took up*

And I hallede to the hokes and the hert smote. *drew back the catches*

And happenyd that I hitt hym byhynde the lefte scholdire,

55 That the blode braste owte appon bothe the sydes; *burst*

And he balkede and brayed and bruschede thurgh the greves, [8]

---

[1] *The second branches (ryalls) extended splendidly from the beam*

[2] *And he finished off with a set of six troches (clusters of points) on the one side and five on the other*

[3] *But there followed him a soar (four-year-old buck) that served him very attentively*

[4] *And at the trunk of a birch tree made my hunting dog lie down*

[5] *Set the stock of my crossbow firmly in position and took aim at the hart*

[6] *And looked cautiously about and sniffed the air eagerly*

[7] *And the soar paused and advanced cautiously and stared all about*

[8] *And he stumbled and bellowed and dashed through the thicket*

As alle had hurlede one ane hepe that in the holte longede. [1]

And sone the sowre that hym sewet resorte to his feris,   *returned; companions*

And thay, forfrayede of his fare, to the fellys thay hyen,   *terrified; moors*

60 And I hyede to my hounde and hent hym up sone,   *hastened; seized*

And louset my lyame and lete hym umbycaste. [2]

The breris and the brakans were blody byronnen;

And he assentis to that sewte and seches hym aftire   *pursuit; gives chase*

There he was crepyde into a krage and crouschede to the erthe. [3]

65 Dede als a dore-nayle doun was he fallen;

And I hym hent by the hede and heryett hym uttire,   *seized; dragged him out*

Turned his troches and tachede thaym into the erthe,   *horns; impaled*

Kest up that keuduart and kutt of his tonge,   *turned over; rascal(?) (see note)*

Brayde owte his bewells my bereselet to fede.   *Drew; bowels*

70 And I slitte hym at the assaye to see how me semyde,   *assay (see note)*

And he was floreschede full faire of two fyngere brede.   *lined with fat; breadth*

I chese to the chawylls chefe to begynn,   *started at; jaws; first of all*

And ritte doun at a rase reghte to the tayle,   *ripped; rush*

And than the herbere anone aftir I makede;   *first stomach soon*

75 I raughte the righte legge byfore, ritt it theraftir.   *grasped; ripped*

And so fro legge to legge I lepe thaym aboute;   *moved quickly*

And the felle fro the fete fayre I departede,   *skin*

And flewe it doun with my fiste faste to the rigge.   *flayed; backbone*

I tighte owte my trenchore and toke of the scholdirs,   *drew; knife*

80 Cuttede corbyns bone and keste it awaye.   *ravens' (see note)*

I slitte hym full sleghely and slyppede in my fyngere,   *skillfully*

Lesse the poynte scholde perche the pawnche or the guttys;   *pierce*

I soughte owte my sewet and semblete it togedire,   *suet; gathered*

And pullede oute the pawnche and putt it in an hole.

85 I grippede owte the guttes and graythede thaym besyde,   *set*

And than the nombles anone name I thereaftire;   *edible innards soon took*

Rent up fro the rygge reghte to the myddis,   *slit; back*

And then the fourches full fayre I fonge fro the sydes,   *haunches; took*

And chynede hym chefely and choppede of the nekke,   *split along the spine; off*

90 And the hede and the haulse homelyde in sondree.   *neck butchered*

---

[1] *As if everything that lived in the wood had been thrown into confusion*

[2] *And loosed my leash and let him (the hound) cast about for the scent*

[3] *Where he (the stag) had crept into a crag and pressed himself down to the earth*

45

The fete of the fourche I feste thurgh the sydis,   *haunch; secured*
And hevede all into ane hole and hidde it with ferne,   *ferns*
With hethe and with horemosse hilde it about,   *heather; hairmoss concealed*
That no fostere of the fee scholde fynde it theraftir;   *forester (see note)*
95   Hid the hornes and the hede in ane hologhe oke,   *hollow*
That no hunte scholde it hent ne have it in sighte.   *hunter; seize*
I foundede faste therefro for ferde to be wryghede,   *hastened; fear; betrayed*
And sett me oute one a syde to see how it chevede   *turned out*
To wayte it frome wylde swyne that wyse bene of nesse.   *keep; nose*
100   And als I satte in my sette the sone was so warme,
And I for slepeles was slome and slomerde a while.   *heavy*
And there me dremed in that dowte a full dreghe swevynn,   *long dream*
And whate I seghe in my saule the sothe I schall telle.   *saw*

I seghe thre thro men threpden full yerne,   *keen; [who] disputed; eagerly*
105   And moted of myche-whate and maden thaym full tale.   *spoke at great length*
And ye will, ledys, me listen ane hande-while,   *listeners; moment*
I schall reken thaire araye redely for sothe,   *tell; dress*
And to yowe neven thaire names naytly thereaftire.   *name; exactly*
The firste was a ferse freke, fayrere than thies othire,   *fierce man*
110   A bolde beryn one a blonke bownne for to ryde,   *knight; steed equipped*
A hathelle on ane heghe horse with hauke appon hande.   *noble man; great*
He was balghe in the breste and brode in the scholdirs,   *bulging*
His axles and his armes were iliche longe,   *shoulders; in like manner*
And in the medill als a mayden menskfully schapen,   *gracefully*
115   Longe legges and large, and lele for to schewe.   *fine*
He streghte hym in his sterapis and stode uprightes;   *stretched; stirrups*
He ne hade no hode ne no hatte bot his here one,   *alone*
A chaplet one his chefelere chosen for the nones,   *garland; head (of hair)*
Raylede alle with rede rose, richeste of floures,   *Adorned*
120   With trayfoyles and trewloves of full triede perles,   *trefoils; love knots; fine*
With a chefe charebocle chosen in the myddes.   *choice carbuncle conspicuous*
He was gerede alle in grene, alle with golde bywevede,   *dressed; interwoven*
Enbroddirde alle with besanttes and beralles full riche;   *gold coins; beryl gems*
His colere with calsydoynnes clustrede full thikke,
125   With many dyamandes full dere dighte one his sleves.   *set*
The semys with saphirs sett were full many,   *seams*
With emeraudes and amatistes appon iche syde,
With full riche rubyes raylede by the hemmes;   *arranged*

46

The price of that perry were worthe powndes full many. — *jewelry*

130 His sadill was of sykamoure that he satt inn,

His bridell alle of brente golde with silke brayden raynes,

His cropoure was of tartaryne that traylede to the erthe; — *crupper; rich silk*

And he throly was threven of thritty yere of elde, — *vigorously*

And therto yonge and yape, and Youthe was his name, — *active*

135 And the semelyeste segge that I seghe ever. — *knight*

The seconde segge in his sete satte at his ese,

A renke alle in rosette that rowmly was schapyn, — *red-brown wool; amply*

In a golyone of graye girde in the myddes, — *tunic*

And iche bagge in his bosome bettir than othere. — *money bag*

140 One his golde and his gude gretly he mousede, — *goods; mused*

His renttes and his reches rekened he full ofte, — *riches*

Of mukkyng, of marlelyng, and mendynge of howses,[1]

Of benes of his bondemen, of benefetis many, — *services; laborers; favors*

Of presanttes of polayle, of pufilis als; — *poultry; small parcels of land*

145 Of purches of ploughe-londes, of parkes full faire,

Of profettis of his pasturs, that his purse mendis; — *increases*

Of stiewardes, of storrours, stirkes to bye, — *storekeepers, heifers*

Of clerkes, of countours, his courtes to holde; — *legal pleaders; manorial courts*

And alle his witt in this werlde was one his wele one.

150 Hym semyde for to see to of sexty yere elde, — *look at*

And therfore men in his marche Medill Elde hym callede. — *region*

The thirde was a laythe lede lenyde one his syde, — *ugly; [who] leant on*

A beryne bownn alle in blake with bedis in his hande,

Croked and courbede, encrampeschett for elde; — *bowed down, contorted*

155 Alle disfygured was his face and fadit his hewe, — *pale*

His berde and browes were blanchede full whitte,

And the hare one his hede hewede of the same. — *hair*

He was ballede and blynde and alle babirlippede, — *bald; thick-lipped*

Totheles and tenefull, I tell yowe for sothe; — *querulous*

160 And ever he momelide and ment and mercy he askede, — *mumbled and moaned*

And cried kenely one Criste and his crede sayde,

With sawtries full sere tymes to sayntes in heven; — *psalteries (psalms); various*

---

[1] *Of fertilizing with manure and marl, and repairing of houses*

Envyous and angrye, and Elde was his name.

I helde hym be my hopynge a hundrethe yeris of age, · *estimate*

165 And bot his cruche and his couche he carede for no more. · *except for*

Now hafe I rekkende yow theire araye redely the sothe, · *told; readily*

And also namede yow thaire names naytly thereaftire, · *exactly*

And now thaire carpynge I sall kythe — knowe it if yowe liste. [1]

Now this gome alle in grene so gayly attyrede,

170 This hathelle one this heghe horse with hauke one his fiste,

He was yonge and yape and yernynge to armes, · *lively; eager for*

And pleynede hym one paramours and peteuosely syghede. [2]

He sett hym up in his sadill and seyde theis wordes:

"My lady, my leman, that I hafe luffede ever, · *lover; always loved*

175 My wele and my wirchip in werlde where thou duellys, · *happiness; devotion*

My playstere of paramours, my lady with pappis full swete, · *healer; breasts*

Alle my hope and my hele, myn herte es thyn ownn! · *health*

I byhete the a heste and heghely I avowe, · *make you a promise; solemnly*

There schall no hode ne no hatt one my hede sitt · *hood; hat; head*

180 Till that I joyntly with a gesserante justede hafe with onere, [3]

And done dedis for thi love, doghety in armes."

Bot then this gome alle in graye greved with this wordes, · *man; complained*

And sayde, "Felowe, be my faythe thou fonnes full yerne, · *by; play the fool*

For alle es fantome and foly that thou with faris. · *deal with*

185 Where es the londe and the lythe that thou arte lorde over? · *people*

For alle thy ryalle araye renttis hase thou none,

Ne for thi pompe and thi pride penyes bot fewe,

For alle thi golde and thi gude gloes one thi clothes, · *glows*

And thou hafe caughte thi kaple thou cares for no fothire. [4]

190 Bye the stirkes with thi stede and stalles thaym make, · *Buy yourself heifers*

Thi brydell of brent golde wolde bullokes the gete,

The pryce of thi perrye wolde purches the londes, · *jewelry; buy for yourself*

---

[1] *And now their debate I shall make known — understand it if you like*

[2] *And made laments about lovers and piteously sighed*

[3] *Until I resolutely in chain mail have jousted with honor*

[4] *And if you've caught your horse you care not for the cart-load (i.e., Youth uses his horse for pleasure, not as a draught animal)*

48

And wonne, wy, in thi witt, for wele neghe thou spilles."[1]

	Than the gome alle in grene greved full sore,	*man*
195	And sayd, "Sir, be my soule, thi counsell es feble.	
	Bot thi golde and thi gude thou hase no god ells;	
	For, be the Lorde and the laye that I leve inne,	*by; faith; believe*
	And by the Gode that me gaffe goste and soule,	*gave spirit*
	Me were levere one this launde lengen a while,	*I would rather; linger*
200	Stoken in my stele-wede one my stede bakke,	*Enclosed; coat of mail*
	Harde haspede in my helme and in my here-wedys,	*buckled; battle attire*
	With a grym grownden glayfe graythely in myn honde,	*sword ready*
	And see a kene knyghte come and cowpe with myselven,	*contend*
	That I myghte halde that I hafe highte and heghely avowede,	*promised*
205	And parfourme my profers and proven my strengthes,	
	Than alle the golde and the gude that thoue gatt ever,	
	Than alle the londe and the lythe that thoue arte lorde over;	*people*
	And ryde to a revere redily thereaftir,	*riverbank*
	With haukes full hawtayne that heghe willen flye,	*proud; high*
210	And when the fewlis bene founden fawkoneres hyenn	*hasten*
	To lache oute thaire lessches and lowsen thaym sone,	*take; loosen*
	And keppyn of thaire caprons and casten fro honde;	*snatch off; hoods*
	And than the hawteste in haste hyghes to the towre,	*rises in soaring flight*
	With theire bellys so brighte blethely thay ryngen,	*gaily*
215	And there they hoven appon heghte as it were heven angelles.	*are poised*
	Then the fawkoners full fersely to floodes thay hyen,	*water courses*
	To the revere with thaire roddes to rere up the fewles,[2]	*(see note)*
	Sowssches thaym full serely to serven thaire hawkes.	*Swishes; vigorously*
	Than tercelettes full tayttely telys doun striken;	*peregrines; swiftly; teal*
220	Laners and lanerettis lightten to thes endes,[3]	
	Metyn with the maulerdes and many doun striken;	*Meet; mallards*
	Fawkons thay founden freely to lighte,	*hasten eagerly; swoop*
	With hoo and howghe to the heron thay hitten hym full ofte,	*ho and huff*
	Buffetyn hym, betyn hym, and brynges hym to sege,	*siege (see note)*
225	And saylen hym full serely and sesyn hym thereaftire.	*attack; separately*

---

[1] *And keep your wits, man, for you're well nigh destroying yourself*

[2] *To the wetlands with their beating rods to flush out the birds*

[3] *Lanners (female) and lannerets (male hawks) swoop down upon ducks (OE* ende)

Then fawkoners full fersely founden tham aftire,   *hastens*

To helpen thaire hawkes thay hyen thaym full yerne,

For the bitt of his bill bitterly he strikes.   *sharp edge; (the heron's) bill*

They knelyn doun one theire knees and krepyn full lowe,

230   Wynnen to his wynges and wrythen thaym togedire,   *twist*

Brosten the bones and brekyn thaym in sondire,

Puttis owte with a penn the maryo one his glove,   *quill; marrow (see note)*

And quopes thaym to the querrye that quelled hym to the dethe. [1]

He quyrres thaym and quotes thaym, quyppeys full lowde, [2]

235   Cheres thaym full chefely ecchekkes to leve,   *Encourages; especially (see note)*

Than henttis thaym one honde and hodes thaym theraftire,   *takes; hoods*

Cowples up theire cowers thaire caprons to holde, [3]

Lowppes in thaire lesses thorowe vertwells of silvere.   *Loops; leashes; rings*

Than he laches to his luyre and lokes to his horse,   *picks up his lure*

240   And lepis upe one the lefte syde als the laghe askes.   *custom*

Portours full pristly putten upe the fowlis,   *Bearers; keenly*

And taryen for theire tercelettis that tenyn thaym full ofte,   *wait; harass*

For some chosen to the echecheke thoghe some chefe bettire.   *go; achieve*

Spanyells full spedily thay spryngen abowte,

245   Bedagged for dowkynge when digges bene enewede; [4]

And than kayre to the courte that I come fro,   *go*

With ladys full lovely to lappyn in myn armes,   *embrace*

And clyp thaym and kysse thaym and comforthe myn hert,   *clasp*

And than with damesels dere to daunsen in thaire chambirs,

250   Riche romance to rede and rekken the sothe   *recount; truth*

Of kempes and of conquerours, of kynges full noblee,   *champions*

How thay wirchipe and welthe wanne in thaire lyves;   *honor*

With renkes in ryotte to revelle in haulle,   *knights*

With coundythes and carolles and compaynyes sere,   *part-songs; various*

255   And chese me to the chesse that chefe es of gamnes: *betake myself*

And this es life for to lede while I schalle lyfe here.

---

[1] *And whoops (calls) them (the hawks) [by swinging the lure] to the quarry (the heron) that has been crushed to death*

[2] *He quarries the hawks (feeds them on the quarry) and gluts them, and whips the rods loudly to direct them (to it)*

[3] *Draws up the leather braces (cowers), in order to hold the hood tight over the falcon's head*

[4] *Muddied from pursuing ducks that had been driven down into the water*

And thou with wandrynge and woo schalte wake for thi gudes,   *restlessness*

And be thou dolven and dede thi dole schall be schorte,   *buried; mourning*

And he that thou leste luffes schall layke hym therewith,   *least love; sport*

260   And spend that thou haste longe sparede, the devyll spede hym els!"   *help*

Than this renke alle in rosett rothelede thies wordes: *croaked angrily*

He sayde, "Thryfte and thou have threpid this thirtene wynter;   *disputed*

I seghe wele samples bene sothe that sayde bene yore: *proverbs*

Fole es that with foles delys; flyte we no lengare."   *Fool; deals; dispute*

265   Than this beryn alle in blake bownnes hym to speke,   *prepares himself*

And sayde, "Sirres, by my soule, sottes bene ye bothe!

Bot will ye hendely me herken ane hande-while,   *courteously*

And I schalle stynte your stryffe and stillen your threpe.   *stop; quarrel*

I sett ensample bi myselfe and sekis it no forthire: *seek*

270   While I was yonge in my youthe and yape of my dedys,   *active*

I was als everrous in armes as outher of youreselven,   *eager for glory; either*

And as styffe in a stourre one my stede bake,   *battle*

And as gaye in my gere als any gome ells,   *dress*

And as lelly byluffede with ladyse and maydens.   *loyally beloved*

275   My likame was lovely, es lothe nowe to schewe,   *body; [which] is ugly*

And as myche wirchip I wane, iwis, as ye bothen.

And aftir irkede me with this and ese was me levere,   *grew tired; preferable*

Als man in his medill elde his makande wolde have.   *comfort*

Than I mukkede and marlede and made up my howses,[1]

280   And purcheste me ploughe-londes and pastures full noble,

Gatte gude and golde full gaynly to honde,   *Got wealth; readily*

Reches and renttes were ryfe to myselven.   *Riches; plenteous*

Bot Elde undireyode me are I laste wiste,   *undermined; before; least suspected*

And alle disfegurede my face and fadide my hewe;

285   Bothe my browes and my berde blawnchede full whitte,

And when he sotted my syghte than sowed myn hert,   *blurred; grieved*

Croked me, cowrbed me, encrampeschet myn hondes,[2]

That I ne may hefe tham to my hede ne noghte helpe myselven,   *raise*

Ne stale stonden one my fete bot I my staffe have.   *Nor stand up; unless*

---

[1] *Then I fertilized with muck and marl and refurbished my estates*

[2] *Made me crooked, bent me low, deformed my hands*

290 Makes youre mirrours bi me, men, bi youre trouthe: *Take me as example*
This schadowe in my schewere schunte ye no while. [1]
And now es dethe at my dore that I drede moste;
I ne wot wiche day ne when ne whate tyme he comes, *don't know which*
Ne whedirwardes, ne whare, ne whatte to do aftire.
295 Bot many modyere than I, men one this molde, *prouder; earth*
Hafe passed the pase that I schall passe sone,
And I schall neven yow the names of nyne of the beste *name you*
That ever wy in this werlde wiste appon erthe, *person; knew*
That were conquerours full kene and kiddeste of other. *brave; most renowned*

300 The firste was Sir Ector and aldeste of tyme,
When Troygens of Troye were tried to fighte
With Menylawse the mody kynge and men out of Grece, *proud*
That thaire cité assegede and sayled it full yerne,
For Elayne his ownn quene that thereinn was halden,
305 That Paresche the proude knyghte paramours lovede. *passionately*
Sir Ectore was everous als the storye telles, *eager*
And als clerkes in the cronycle cownten the sothe: *relate*
Nowmbron thaym to nynetene and nyne mo by tale *They reckon*
Of kynges with crounes he killede with his handes,
310 And full fele other folke, als ferly were ellis. *many; strange*
Then Achilles his adversarye undide with his werkes,
With wyles and no wirchipe woundede hym to dethe *honor*
Als he tentid to a tulke that he tuke of were. *was tending; man; in*
And he was slayne for that slaughte sleghely theraftir *(i.e., Achilles); slaughter*
315 With the wyles of a woman as he had wroghte byfore.
Than Menylawse the mody kynge hade myrthe at his hert,
That Ectore hys enymy siche auntoure hade fallen, *chance*
And with the Gregeis of Grece he girde over the walles, *Greeks; rushed*
The prowde paleys dide he pulle doun to the erthe,
320 That was rialeste of araye and rycheste undir the heven. *most royal*
And then the Trogens of Troye teneden full sore, *grieved*
And semblen thaym full serely and sadly thay foughten. *individually*
Bot the lure at the laste lighte appon Troye, *disaster*
For there Sir Priamus the prynce put was to dethe,

---

[1] *Never shrink from this reflection [or] foreshadowing [of death] in my mirror*

52

325	And Pantasilia the quene paste hym byfore.	*died*
	Sir Troylus, a trewe knyghte that tristyly hade foghten,	*faithfully*
	Neptolemus, a noble knyghte at nede that wolde noghte fayle,	
	Palamedes, a prise knyghte and preved in armes,	*excellent; proven*
	Ulixes and Ercules, that full everrous were bothe,	*eager*
330	And other fele of that ferde fared of the same,	*many others; company*
	As Dittes and Dares demeden togedir.	*declared*
	Aftir this Sir Alysaunder alle the worlde wanne,	
	Bothe the see and the sonde and the sadde erthe,	*sand; solid*
	The iles of the Oryent to Ercules boundes —	
335	Ther Ely and Ennoke ever hafe bene sythen,	
	And to the come of Antecriste unclosede be thay never —	*coming; released*
	And conquered Calcas knyghtly theraftire,	*Colchis*
	Ther jentille Jazon the Grewe wane the flese of golde.	*Where*
	Then grathede he hym to Gadres the gates full righte,	*prepared; ways; directly*
340	And there Sir Gadyfere the gude the Gaderayns assemblet,	*people of Gadres*
	And rode oute full ryally to rescowe the praye;	*booty*
	And than Emenyduse hym mete and made hym full tame,	
	And girdes Gadyfere to the grounde, gronande full sore,	*strikes*
	And there that doughty was dede and mekill dole makede.	*great (see note)*
345	Then Alixander the Emperour, that athell kynge hymselven,	*noble*
	Arayed hym for to ryde with the renkes that he hade:	
	Ther was the mody Meneduse, a mane of Artage —	*Arcadia*
	He was Duke of that douth and a dussypere —	*army; one of twelve peers*
	Sir Filot and Sir Florydase, full ferse men of armes,	
350	Sir Clyton and Sir Caulus, knyghtis full noble,	
	And Sir Garsyene the gaye, a gude man of armes,	
	And Sir Lyncamoure thaym ledys with a lighte will.	
	And than Sir Cassamus thaym kepide, and the kyng prayede	*detained*
	To fare into Fesome his frendis to helpe;	*Epheson (see note)*
355	For one Carrus the kynge was comen owte of Inde,	
	And hade Fozome affrayede and Fozayne asegede	*alarmed; besieged*
	For Dame Fozonase the faire that he of lufe bysoughte.	
	The kynge agreed hym to goo and graythed hym sone,	*prepared*
	In mendys of Amenyduse that he hade mysdone. [1]	

---

[1] *To make amends for what Emenidus had done amiss*

360	Then ferde he towarde Facron and by the flode abydes,	
	And there he tighte up his tentis and taried there a while.	*set up*
	There knyghtis full kenely caughten theire leve	*took*
	To fare into Fozayne Dame Fozonase to see,	
	And Idores and Edease all bydene;	*all together*
365	And there Sir Porus and his prynces to the poo avowede.	*peacock made vows*
	Was never speche byfore spoken sped bettir aftir,	*fared*
	For als thay demden to doo thay deden full even.	
	For there Sir Porus the prynce into the prese thrynges,	*thick of battle goes*
	And bare the batelle one bake and abaschede thaym swythe.	*returned blows*
370	And than the bolde Bawderayne bowes to the kyng,	*goes*
	And brayde owte the brighte brande owt of the kynges hande,	*drew; sword*
	And Florydase full freschely foundes hym aftir,	*hastens*
	And hent the helme of his hede and the halse crakede.	*neck*
	Than Sir Gadefere the gude gripis his axe,	
375	And into the Indyans ofte auntirs hym sone,	*ventures*
	And thaire stiffe standerte to stikkes he hewes.	*standard*
	And than Sir Cassamus the kene Carrus releves:	
	When he was fallen appon fote he fet hym his stede.	*fetched; horse*
	And aftyr that Sir Cassamus Sir Carus he drepitt,	*slew*
380	And for that poynte Sir Porus perset hym to dethe.	*feat of arms; pierced*
	And than the Indyans ofte uttire tham droghen,	*withdrew into the open*
	And fledden faste of the felde and Alexandere suede.	*followed*
	When thay were skaterede and skayled and skyftede in sondere, [1]	
	Alyxandere oure athell kyng ames hym to lenge,	*resolves to stay*
385	And fares into Fozayne festes to make,	*Epheson*
	And weddis wy unto wy that wilnede togedire.	*person to person*
	Sir Porus the pryce knyghte moste praysed of othere	*noble*
	Fonge Fozonase to fere, and fayne were thay bothe;	*Took*
	The bolde Bawderayne of Baderose, Sir Cassayle hymselven,	
390	Bele Edyas the faire birde bade he no nother;	*Beautiful; woman*
	And Sir Betys the beryne the beste of his tyme,	
	Idores his awnn lufe aughte he hymselven;	*own; obtained*
	Then iche lede hade the love that he hade longe yernede.	*each person*
	Sir Alixander oure Emperour ames hym to ryde,	*resolves to go*
395	And bewes towardes Babyloyne with the beryns that were levede,	*turns; left*

---

[1] *When they were scattered and dispersed and divided asunder*

Bycause of Dame Candace that comforthed hym moste;
And that cité he bysegede and assayllede it aftire,
While hym the gatis were yete and yolden the keyes.   *Until; surrendered*
And there that pereles prynce was puysonede to dede,   *poisoned*
400   Thare he was dede of a drynke, as dole es to here,   *hear*
That the curssede Cassander in a cowpe hym broghte.
He conquered with conqueste kyngdomes twelve,
And dalte thaym to his dussypers when he the dethe tholede;   *divided; suffered*
And thus the worthieste of this werlde went to his ende.

405   Thane Sir Sezere hymselven, that Julyus was hatten,   *Caesar*
Alle Inglande he aughte at his awnn will,
When the Bruyte in his booke Bretayne it callede.
The trewe toure of Londone in his tyme he makede,
And craftely the condithe he compaste thereaftire,   *aqueduct; wrought*
410   And then he droghe hym to Dovire and duellyde there a while,   *withdrew*
And closede ther a castelle with cornells full heghe,   *battlements*
Warnestorede it full wiesely, als witnesses the sothe,   *Provisioned; prudently*
For there es hony in that holde holden sythen his tyme.
Than rode he into Romayne and rawnsede it sone,
415   And Cassabalount the kynge conquerede thereaftire.
Then graythed he hym into Grece and gete hym belyve;   *quickly*
The semely cité Alexaunder seside he theraftire;   *of Alexandria*
Affrike and Arraby and Egipt the noble,
Surry and Sessoyne sessede he togedir,   *Syria; Saxony*
420   With alle the iles of the see appon iche a syde.
Thies thre were paynymes full priste and passed alle othire.   *esteemed*

Of thre Jewes full gentill jugge we aftir,   *let us consider*
In the Olde Testament as the storye tellis,
In a booke of the Bible that breves of kynges,   *tells*
425   And renkes that rede kane Regum it callen.   *Book of Kings*
The firste was gentill Josue that was a Jewe noble,
Was heryet for his holynes into hevenriche.   *carried off*
When Pharaoo had flayede the folkes of Israelle,   *put to flight*
Thay ranne into the Rede See for radde of hymselven,   *fear*
430   And than Josue the Jewe Jhesu he prayed
That the peple myghte passe unpereschede that tyme.
And than the see sett up appon sydes twayne,

	In manere of a mode walle that made were with hondes,	*mud*
	And thay soughten over the see sownnde alle togedir.	*went; safe*
435	And Pharaoo full fersely folowede thaym aftire,	
	And efte Josue the Jewe Jhesus he prayede,	
	And the see sattillede agayne and sanke thaym thereinn —	*settled*
	A soppe for the Sathanas; unsele have theire bones!	*sop; misfortune*
	And aftire Josue the Jewe full gentilly hym bere,	
440	And conquerede kynges and kyngdomes twelve,	
	And was a conqueroure full kene and moste kyd in his tyme.	*renowned*
	Than David the doughty thurghe Drightynes sonde	*God's dispensation*
	Was caughte from kepyng of schepe and a kyng made.	
	The grete grym Golyas he to grounde broghte	
445	And sloughe hym with his slynge and with no sleghte ells.	*trickery*
	The stone thurghe his stele helme stong into his brayne,	*struck*
	And he was dede of that dynt — the Devyll hafe that reche!	*him who cares*
	And than was David full dere to Drightyn hymselven,	
	And was a prophete of pryse and praysed full ofte.	*worth*
450	Bot yit greved he his God gretely theraftire,	
	For Urye his awnn knyghte in aventure he wysede	*Uriah; peril; sent*
	There he was dede at that dede, as dole es to here;	
	For Bersabee his awnn birde was alle that bale rerede.	*evil-doing done*
	The gentill Judas Machabee was a Jewe kene,	
455	And thereto worthy in were and wyse of his dedis.	*battle*
	Antiochus and Appolyne aythere he drepide,	*slew*
	And Nychanore, another kynge, full naytly thereaftire,	*dexterously*
	And was a conquerour kydde and knawen with the beste.	
	Thies thre were Jewes full joly and justers full noble,	*jousters*
460	That full loughe have bene layde sythen gane full longe tyme:	*low*
	Of siche doughety doers looke what es worthen.	*become*
	Of the thre Cristen to carpe couthely thereaftir,	
	That were conquerours full kene and kyngdomes wonnen,	
	Areste was Sir Arthure and eldeste of tyme,	*First*
465	For alle Inglande he aughte at his awnn will,	
	And was kynge of this kythe and the crowne hade.	*country*
	His courte was at Carlele comonly holden,	
	With renkes full ryalle of his Rownnde Table,	
	That Merlyn with his maystries made in his tyme,	*magical powers*

470	And sett the Sege Perilous so semely one highte,	*(see note)*
	There no segge scholde sitt bot hym scholde schame tyde,	
	Owthir dethe withinn the thirde daye demed to hymselven,	*Or*
	Bot Sir Galade the gude that the gree wanne.	*supreme reward won*
	There was Sir Launcelot de Lake full lusty in armes,	
475	And Sir Gawayne the gude that never gome harmede,	
	Sir Askanore, Sir Ewayne, Sir Errake Fytz Lake,	*Eric, son of King Lac*
	And Sir Kay the kene and kyd of his dedis,	
	Sir Percevalle de Galeys that preved had bene ofte,	*Wales*
	Mordrede and Bedwere, men of mekyll myghte,	*great*
480	And othere fele of that ferde, folke of the beste.	*company*
	Then Roystone the riche kyng, full rakill of his werkes,	*rash*
	He made a blyot to his bride of the berdes of kynges,	*robe for*
	And aughtilde Sir Arthures berde one scholde be;	*intended*
	Bot Arthure oure athell kynge another he thynkes,	
485	And faughte with hym in the felde till he was fey worthen.	*dead*
	And than Sir Arthure oure kyng ames hym to ryde;	
	Uppon Sayn Michaells Mounte mervaylles he wroghte,	
	There a dragone he dreped that drede was full sore.	*slew*
	And than he sayled over the see into sere londes,	*various*
490	Whils alle the beryns of Bretayne bewede hym to fote.	*Until; bowed down*
	Gascoyne and Gyane gatt he thereaftir,	*Gascony; Guienne*
	And conquered kyngdomes and contrees full fele.	
	Than ames he into Inglonde into his awnn kythe;	*goes*
	The gates towardes Glassthenbery full graythely he rydes.	*ways; promptly*
495	And ther Sir Mordrede hym mett by a more syde,	
	And faughte with hym in the felde to alle were fey worthen,	*until*
	Bot Arthur oure athell kyng and Wawayne his knyghte.	
	And when the felde was flowen and fey bot thaymselven,	
	Than Arthure Sir Wawayne athes by his trouthe	*adjures*
500	That he swiftely his swerde scholde swynge in the mere,	*sea*
	And whatt selcouthes he see the sothe scholde he telle.	*marvels*
	And Sir Wawayne swith to the swerde and swange it in the mere,	*quickly*
	And ane hande by the hiltys hastely it grippes,	
	And brawndeschet that brighte swerde and bere it awaye.	
505	And Wawayne wondres of this werke, and wendes bylyve	*quickly*
	To his lorde there he hym lefte, and lokes abowte,	
	And he ne wiste in alle this werlde where he was bycomen.	
	And then he hyghes hym in haste and hedis to the mere,	

And seghe a bote from the banke and beryns thereinn.
510 Thereinn was Sir Arthure and othire of his ferys,   *companions*
And also Morgn la Faye that myche couthe of sleghte.   *had knowledge of*
And there ayther segge seghe othir laste, for sawe he hym no more.   *warrior*

Sir Godfraye de Bolenn siche grace of God hade
That alle Romanye he rode and rawnnsunte it sone;   *(?) a region in Asia Minor*
515 The Amorelle of Antyoche aftire he drepit,   *Emir*
That was called Corborant, kiluarde of dedis;   *infamous*
And aftir he was callede kynge and the crownn hade
Of Jerasalem and of the Jewes gentill togedir,
And with the wirchipe of this werlde he went to his ende.

520 Than was Sir Cherlemayne chosen chefe kynge of Fraunce,
With his doghty doussypers, to do als hym lykede;
Sir Rowlande the riche and Duke Raynere of Jene,   *(see note)*
Olyver and Aubrye and Ogere Deauneys,
And Sir Naymes at the nede that never wolde fayle,
525 Turpyn and Terry, two full tryed lordes,
And Sir Sampsone hymselfe of the Mounte Ryalle,
Sir Berarde de Moundres, a bolde beryn in armes,   *Berard de Mondisdier*
And gud Sir Gy de Burgoyne, full gracyous of dedis;   *Burgundy*
The katur fitz Emowntez were kydde knyghtes alle,   *four sons of Aymon*
530 And other moo than I may myne or any man elles.   *remember*
And then Sir Cherlles the chefe ches for to ryde,
And paste towardes Polborne to proven his strenghte;   *Paderborn (in Saxony)*
Salamadyne the Sowdane he sloghe with his handis,
And that cité he bysegede and saylede it full ofte,
535 While hym his yernynge was yett and the gates opynede;   *Until; granted*
And Witthyne thaire waryed kynge wolde nott abyde, [1]
Bot soghte into Sessoyne socoure hym to gete;   *Saxony*
And Cherlemayne oure chefe kynge cheses into the burgh,   *goes*
And Dame Nioles anone he name to hymselven,   *took*
540 And maried hir to Maundevyle that scho hade myche lovede;
And spedd hym into hethyn Spayne spedely thereaftire,
And fittilled hym by Flagott faire for to loge.   *prepared; river Flagot; lodge*

---

[1] *And Widukund (a Saxon chief) their accursed king would not submit*

	There Olyver the everous aunterde hymselven,	*eager ventured*
	And faughte with Sir Ferambrace and fonge hym one were;	*captured*
545	And than they fologhed hym in a fonte and Florence hym callede.	*baptized*
	And than moved he hym to Mawltryple Sir Balame to seche,	*Mautrible*
	And that Emperour at Egremorte aftir he takes,	*(i.e., Balan); Aigremont*
	And wolde hafe made Sir Balame a man of oure faythe,	
	And garte feche forthe a founte by-fore-with his eghne,	*caused*
550	And he dispysede it and spitte and spournede it to the erthe,	*he (Balan); kicked*
	And one swyftely with a swerde swapped of his hede.	
	And Dame Floripe the faire was cristened thereaftire,	
	And kende thaym to the corownne that Criste had one hede,	*guided*
	And the nayles anone nayttly thereaftire,	*fittingly*
555	When he with passyoun and pyne was naylede one the rode.	
	And than those relikes so riche redely he takes,	
	And at Sayne Denys he thaym dide, and duellyd there forever.	*placed*
	And than bodworde unto Merchill full boldly he sendys,	*message*
	And bade hym Cristyne bycome and one Criste leve,	
560	Or he scholde bette doun his borowes and brenn hym thereinn;	
	And garte Genyone goo that erande that grevede thaym alle.	*caused Ganelon*
	Thane rode he to Rowncyvale, that rewed hym aftire,	
	There Sir Rowlande the ryche Duke refte was his lyfe,	
	And Olyver his awnn fere that ay had bene trewe,	
565	And Sir Turpyn the trewe that full triste was at nede,	*trusty*
	And full fele othir folke, als ferly were elles.	*wondrous*
	Then suede he the Sarazenes seven yere and more,	*pursued*
	And the Sowdane at Saragose full sothely he fyndis,	
	And there he bett downn the burghe and Sir Merchill he tuke,	
570	And that daye he dide hym to the dethe als he had wele servede.	*deserved*
	Bot by than his wyes were wery and woundede full many,	*soldiers*
	And he fared into France to fongen thaire riste,	
	And neghede towarde Nerbone, that noyede thaym full sore.	*Narbonne; annoyed*
	And that cité he asseggede appone sere halfves,	*all sides*
575	While hym the gates were yette and yolden the keyes,	*surrendered*
	And Emorye made Emperour even at that tyme,	*Aymeri de Narbonne*
	To have and to holde it to hym and to his ayers.	*heirs*
	And then thay ferden into Fraunce to fongen thaire ese,	*take*
	And at Sayn Denys he dyede at his dayes tyme.	
580	Now hafe I nevened yow the names of nyne of the beste	
	That ever were in this werlde wiste appon erthe,	*known*

And the doghtyeste of dedis in thaire dayes tyme,
Bot doghetynes when dede comes ne dare noghte habyde. [1]

Of wyghes that were wyseste will ye now here,
585 And I schall schortly yow schewe and schutt me ful sone.   *conclude*
Arestotle he was arste in Alexander tyme,
And was a fyne philozophire and a fynour noble,   *alchemist; refiner of metals*
The grete Alexander to graythe and gete golde when hym liste, [2]
And multiplye metalles with mercurye watirs,   *transmute*
590 And with his ewe ardaunt and arsneke pouders,   *ardent spirit (alcohol)*
With salpetir and sal-jeme and siche many othire,   *sal-gem (a gem-like salt)*
And menge his metalles and make fyne silvere,   *mix*
And was a blaunchere of the beste thurgh blaste of his fyre.   *refiner*
Then Virgill thurgh his vertus verrayle he maket   *powers; verily*
595 Bodyes of brighte brasse full boldely to speke,
To telle whate betydde had and whate betyde scholde,   *had happened*
When Dioclesyane was dighte to be dere Emperour;   *ordained*
Of Rome and of Romanye the rygalté he hade.

Than Sir Salomon hymselfe sett hym by hym one;   *set himself apart*
600 His bookes in the Bible bothe bene togedirs.
That one of wisdome and of witt wondirfully teches;
His sampills and his sawes bene sett in the tother: *sayings*
And he was the wyseste in witt that ever wonnede in erthe,   *lived*
And his techynges will bene trowede whills the werlde standes,   *believed*
605 Bothe with kynges and knyghtis and kaysers therinn.

Merlyn was a mervayllous man and made many thynges,
And naymely nygromancye nayttede he ofte,   *practiced*
And graythed Galyan a boure to kepe hyr therin,   *prepared*
That no wy scholde hir wielde ne wynne from hymselven.   *possess*
610 Theis were the wyseste in the worlde of witt that ever yitt were,
Bot dethe wondes for no witt to wende were hym lykes.   *hesitates*

Now of the prowdeste in presse that paramoures loveden

---

[1] *But when death comes doughtiness (prowess, valor) dares not abide*
[2] *To prepare and produce gold for the great Alexander when it pleased him*

	I schalle titly yow telle and tary yow no lengere.	*quickly*
	Amadase and Edoyne in erthe are thay bothe,	
615	That in golde and in grene were gaye in thaire tyme;	
	And Sir Sampsone hymselfe full savage of his dedys,	
	And Dalyda his derelynge, now dethe has tham bothe.	
	Sir Ypomadonn de Poele full priste in his armes,	*(see note); keen*
	The faire Fere de Calabre, now faren are they bothe.	*departed*
620	Generides the gentill full joly in his tyme,	
	And Clarionas that was so clere, are bothe nowe bot erthe.	
	Sir Eglamour of Artas full everous in armes,	*Artois*
	And Cristabelle the clere maye es crept in hir grave,	*pure maiden*
	And Sir Tristrem the trewe, full triste of hymselven,	*trusty*
625	And Ysoute his awnn lufe, in erthe are thay bothe.	
	Whare es now Dame Dido was qwene of Cartage?	
	Dame Candace the comly was called quene of Babyloyne?	
	Penelopie that was price and passed alle othere,	*excellent*
	And Dame Gaynore the gaye, nowe graven are thay bothen,	*Guinevere*
630	And othere moo than I may mene or any man elles.	*tell of*
	Sythen doughtynes when dede comes ne dare noghte habyde,	
	Ne dethe wondes for no witt to wende where hym lykes,	*hesitates*
	And therto paramours and pride puttes he full lowe,	
	Ne there es reches ne rent may rawnsone your lyves,	*riches*
635	Ne noghte es sekire to youreselfe in certayne bot dethe,	*certain*
	And he es so uncertayne that sodaynly he comes,	*unpredictable*
	Me thynke the wele of this werlde worthes to noghte.	*comes to nothing*
	Ecclesiastes the clerke declares in his booke	
	Vanitas vanitatum et omnia vanitas,	*Eccl. 1:2, 12:8*
640	That alle es vayne and vanytes and vanyte es alle.	
	Forthi amendes youre mysse whills ye are men here,	*Therefore; sin*
	Quia in inferno nulla est redempcio —	*Job 7:9*
	For in Helle es no helpe, I hete yow for sothe.	*tell*
	Als God in his gospelle graythely yow teches,	*aptly*
645	*Ite ostendite vos sacerdotibus,*	*Luke 17:14*
	To schryve yow full schirle and schewe yow to prestis.	*completely*
	Et ecce omnia munda sunt vobis,	*Luke 11:41*
	And ye that wronge wroghte schall worthen full clene.	
	Thou man in thi medill elde hafe mynde whate I saye!	
650	I am thi sire and thou my sone, the sothe for to telle,	

And he the sone of thiselfe, that sittis one the stede,
For Elde es sire of Midill Elde, and Midill Elde of Youthe.
And haves gud daye, for now I go — to grave moste me wende.
Dethe dynges one my dore, I dare no lengare byde." *knocks*

655   When I had lenged and layne a full longe while,
I herde a bogle one a bonke be blowen full lowde. *by the river*
And I wakkened therwith and waytted me umbe. *looked around me*
Than the sone was sett and syled full loughe, *sunk; low*
And I founded appon fote and ferkede towarde townn. *hastened; went*
660   And in the monethe of Maye thies mirthes me tydde, *befell me*
Als I schurtted me in a schelfe in the schawes faire, *amused; bank*
And belde me in the birches with bewes full smale, *sheltered myself; boughs*
And lugede me in the leves that lighte were and grene. *lodged*
There dere Drightyne this daye dele us of thi blysse, *May precious God*
665   And Marie that es mylde qwene amende us of synn. Amen Amen.

Thus Endes the Thre Ages.

Explanatory Notes

T=Thornton MS (copy text for this edition); W=the fragmentary Ware MS; G=Gollancz; O=Offord's Early English Text Society edition; T-P=Turville-Petre's 1989 edition.

1ff.   As in *Wynnere*, the opening description of a May morning in the woods creates a sense of transience. See Peck and Waldron.

4–5   The season for hunting deer in medieval England almost certainly began in May, as it did in France (O). Hunting was often a metaphor for the pursuit of love; it also was a conventional prologue to dream visions. A much less common tradition associates the hunters mentioned in Jeremiah 16:16 with prelates who hunt men to make them holy. Of special note here is the fact that the narrator is clearly a poacher (see Peck [1972], Scattergood [1983], and Waldron [1972]). Simply having a bow and arrows or a dog in the forest made a person liable to prosecution; the normal punishment for poaching was a fine or imprisonment.

9–10   The flowers mentioned here, though conventionally associated with Spring, may imply more. Boccaccio, Lydgate, and Skelton all associate the primrose with shortness of life. The periwinkle was identified with death; the *piliole,* or woodland mint, was commended for its medicinal qualities in medieval herbals; and the daisy was a symbol of faithful love of Christ in scriptural exegesis. For Lampe (1973), the flowers balance fleshly excess with its renunciation, thus preparing for the debate.

13–14   Both the cuckoo and the wood-pigeon (*cowschote*) were traditionally associated with Spring; the cuckoo, however, was thought to be unnatural in its rejection of all love, while the cushat, being a dove, was thought to be too lusty. Lampe (1973) connects the cuckoo with Medill Elde, the wood-pidgeon with Youthe. On the contending thrushes, see *Wynnere*, line 37.

17ff.   Like the flowers and birds, animals mentioned may carry metaphorical overtones. The fox was a symbol of fraudulence; the polecat *(filmarte)* emblemized viciousness; the hare, lust. In some traditions, the stag and its soar were exemplars of virtuous conduct; in others, the stag stood for longevity of life.

17   *gouen.* A difficult word. I follow O in deriving it from a form of *gaw,* "to gape or stare at." It could also be a form of "give," in the sense of "devote oneself to." T-P emends to *gon.* G glosses "betook themselves."

19–20   Compare *Wynnere,* line 14.

21ff.   Descriptions of deer hunts are common in the alliterative poems: making the hunter a poacher is not (see Peck, Scattergood [1983], and Whitney). This description has been often praised for its technical precision and for its use of many realistic details. In the following notes, I rely mainly on O's explanation of technical terms, which generally are derived from medieval hunting treatises.

26   *unburneschede.* Deer burnish their antlers against trees to rub off the light skin that coats them. Burnished antlers have reached their final stage of growth for the season.

     beme. The main horn, from which the antlers spring.

27   *feetur.* A growing antler or tine; *as thi fote* suggests their massiveness.

     forfrayed. "Fraying" is the raggedy effect of the shedding skin during the burnishing process. *Forfrayed* means polished clean.

28–30   The tine nearest the head is the "antler," the next above it is the "royal," the third is the "surroyal." At the end of each tine are the *troches* (line 67), the points by which the head (size and age) of the hart is reckoned.

31   *assommet.* A hart was "summed" when its horns were fully formed for that season.

34   *sowre.* A soar was a four-year-old male deer. Older stags often train younger male deer to act as their "squires," watching for danger and providing a decoy during the chase. See George Turbervile's *Book of Hunting,* p. 238: "A Bucke is called the first yeare a Fawne, the second a Pricket, the third a Sorell, the

fourth a Sore, the fifth a Bucke of the first head, and the sixth a Bucke" (as cited by O, pp. 37–38).

39   *berselett*. A dog used specifically for hunting with a bow.

44   *tylere*. The main beam of the cross-bow; it had a groove to guide the arrow, and a mechanism for holding and releasing the cord (O).

53   *hallede to the hokes*. "Drew back the catches (hooks)," thus releasing the bowstring. See *The Master of Game*, ed. William A. and F. Baillie-Grohman (1909; rpt. New York: AMS, 1974), the appendix on "Arms of the Chase," for types of crossbows used in hunting during the fourteenth century.

66–99   For other accounts of the brittling of a deer, see *Sir Gawain and the Green Knight*, lines 1323–64, and *Sir Tristrem*, lines 452–515.

68   *keuduart*. *MED* derives this from French *culvert*, "treacherous"; compare *kiluarde* at line 516. O suggests "rascal," both in its normal sense and in the technical sense of a young deer, usually not yet fit to hunt or eat.

     tonge. The tongue was a great delicacy reserved for the leader of the chase.

69   *owte*. Omitted in T. Supplied by G, O, and T-P.

70   *I slitte hym at the assaye*. T: *sisilte*; G: *scliste*. I follow O's emendation. The *assaye* refers to a part of the breast where the deer's flesh is tested.

74   To "make the arber" was to remove the first stomach, empty it, fill it with blood and fat from the paunch, and then sew it up.

80   *corbyns bone*. A small piece of gristle thrown to crows or ravens for good luck. O (p. 41) cites *The Boke of St. Albans* on this practice:

> Than take owt the shulderis and slytteth a noon
> The baly to the syde from the corbyn bone
> That is corbyns fee: at the deeth he will be.

84   *pawnche*. T: *pawche*.

94   *fostere of the fee*. A forester who held his office by legal inheritance.

104ff.   The "thre thro men" the dreamer sees are the Three Ages. The division of life into stages ultimately goes back to Aristotle (*Rhetoric*, 2.12-14 and *Generation of the Animals*, 10.18), for whom middle age was the pivotal phase of development, youth leading to it, old age declining from it. The number of ages, however, varied from as many as ten to as few as two. For most writers there were either seven or four ages; in the Middle Ages, four was far more popular than three.

        No matter the division, each age was always characterized by typical qualities. Youth was a time of extravagance and general irresponsibility, when one loved hunting and was inclined to lust (according to Horace and Cicero, both authorities in the Middle Ages); Middle Age's conservatism, ambitions, and avarice are well documented in medieval sermons and popular lyrics of the fourteenth and fifteenth centuries, as are Old Age's loquacity, quarrelsomeness, anger, and envy. Other, less common traditions, one should note, stressed the wisdom of Old Age, and the reverence it should be shown.

        In scriptural commentary, the division of life into three ages generally served to stress how brief life is on earth; consequently, these writers emphasized the need to prepare to face God. Some authors connected the three ages with the three watches which Luke (12:37–40) says the faithful keep for Christ's coming, others with the ages mentioned in the Parable of the Sowers (Matt. 13:8; see below note to lines 133ff.). For a general introduction, see Burrow (1988) and Coffman (1934), Lampe (1973), Rowland (1975), Turville-Petre (1977). Further information about Youthe, Medill Elde, and Elde will be given at the appropriate points in the notes.

105   *moted*. T: *moten*.

106   *ane hande-while*. T-P follows G and emends to *a litell while*.

109ff.   The depiction of Youthe here and in his speeches has been praised for its vitality; a number of readers have noted that although youth's excesses are uniformly condemned in moralistic tradition, Youthe seems entirely approved of in the poem.

120ff.   Alliterative poets often ornamented their descriptions of clothing with lists of gems; for the suggestion that Youthe's costume reflects the actual fashions of the later fourteenth century, see Lewis (1968).

130   Medieval saddles were generally made of wood and often richly painted (O).

132   *cropoure.* G emends to *trapoure* to maintain alliteration; T-P agrees. O calls the emendation unnecessary.

133ff.   The ages of Youthe, Medill Elde, and Elde have received much comment; medieval tradition usually put thirty closer to middle age than to youth. Many sources designate old age as between forty and sixty. Rowland (1975) argues that the ages of the debaters, thirty, sixty, and one hundred respectively, reflects scriptural commentary on the Parable of the Sowers (Matt. 13:8), in which these ages are typically assigned to the stages of life and concomitant degrees of spiritual perfection. For Peck they mark the extremity of each age to keep us "mindful of the inevitability of each one's passing to the next degree" (1972, p. 338).

135   *semelyeste.* T: *semely.*

136ff.   Medill Elde has not generally been well thought of by modern readers. For Moran (1978), however, he represents the economic activities of the aristocracy in the aftermath of the Black Death: as they did, Medill Elde farms out desmense lands, is concerned about the collecting of rents, and is very involved in the many particulars of managing his estate. To Moran, Medill Elde's greedy preoccupation, more than what he actually does, is the object of the poem's satire.

137   Medill Elde wears workaday clothes.

147–48   *stiewardes.* T: *stiewarde.* A steward ran his lord's estate. A *storrour* is a store-keeper, such as Chaucer's Reeve (see *The Canterbury Tales* I.597–99). A *countour* is the lord's auditor who presided over the manorial court. He was sometimes assisted by *clerkes.*

158   In *Piers Plowman* B.5.190, Avarice is similarly described.

166   *I.* Omitted in T.

173   *seyde.* T: *seyden.*

180   *with onere.* T omits *with.* O's emendation. G emends to *hafe ones.*

184   *es.* Omitted in T. G follows T.

190–93   See *Wynnere,* lines 288–93.

209–45   Like the brittling of the deer, this account of hawking is fully described and technically precise; knowledge of both were perquisites of nobility. Again I follow O's explanation of technical terms.

212   Hawks were hooded when they were not in flight.

214   Bells of different tones were attached to the back of each leg of the falcon to enable them to be heard even when they could not be seen.

218   *Sowssches.* A term from falconry, meaning "to drive into the air."

          serven: to drive the quarry out of the covert for the hawk.

223   *With hoo and howghe.* Traditional cries to rouse game from cover.

224   *brynges hym to sege.* Since the heron, being a larger bird, may sustain several strikes from the falcon before it is downed, it is as if it were under siege. But T-P's gloss on the phrase, namely to "drive him to the ground," offers the better sense. As he notes, "The 'siege' is 'the station of a heron on the watch for prey' (*OED*, 2c). The action of these lines is described by George Turbervile, *The Booke of Faulconrie or Hauking* (1574, p. 164): 'As soone as the Hearon leaueth the siege, off with hir [the falcon's] hood, and let hir flee: and if shee climb to the Hearon, and beate hir so that she bring hir downe, runne in apase to reskewe hir [the falcon], thrusting the Hearons bil into the grownd and breaking hir winges and legges" (p. 79). The danger is that the heron, on the ground, might harm the hawk with its pointed beak.

226   The transcription of the poem in the Ware MS begins here.

228   *For the bitt.* W: *For wiþ the butte.* T-P: *For with the bitt.*

231   The heron's wings were twisted to prevent them from injuring the hawk.

232   *maryo.* The marrow was traditionally the hawk's reward. Here the falconer serves his bird from his glove. It is not likely the poet would have used another

word, even though this gives his line an *aa/xx* alliterative pattern. G emends *maryo* to *pyth*.

233   *quopes*. T: *quotes*; W: *whopis*. The whoop was a signal for the falcon to come into her quarry.

234   *quyrres*. W: *wharris*. To quarry means to let the hawk feed on the quarry.

         quotes. O glosses as "poss. gluts," citing *OED sv quate, quet*. T-P cites *MED*, which lists the verb under both *houten*, "shout to," and *quaten*, "make calm." The latter sense is preferable.

235   *Cheres thaym*. T: *cheresche hym*. Although *MED* records an instance from 1415 of *cherish* meaning "to coax an animal" (5b), the faultiness of the grammar supports emending to *cheres thaym*. W: *He cheris þem*.

         ecchekkes. The "check" is any unfit bird, such as a dove or crow, which the hawk attacks instead of its intended prey.

238   *vertwells*. These "varvels," on which the owner's name was often engraved, were little silver rings attached to the "jess," a short strap of leather attached to each of the falcon's legs.

239   *luyre*. The bait for recalling hawks.

245   *Bedagged*. Garments were often "dagged" in the fourteenth century, which meant their edges were slashed into long pointed pendants (O).

252   *thay*. T: *thaire*.

254   *coundythes*. The "condut" was a part-song, usually with three voices. Like the carol, it was frequently accompanied by dancing.

260   *thou haste long sparede*. W: *þou sparid;* T-P and G follow W.

261   *rothelede*. W: *ratlid*. O notes that the word in T possibly could mean "counsel, advise."

263   It is possible the word "full" preceding "yore" has been dropped from T. W reads *ful yore*; G, O, and T-P follow W.

280   *ploughe-londes*. Approximately 120 acres (O).

296   *Hafe passed the pase*. On death as a pass from which there is no turning back see Dante, *Inferno*, Canto 1, lines 26–27: *"lo passo / che non lasciò già mai persona viva."*

300   *firste*. T-P emends to *arste*.

300ff.   The purpose and appropriateness of Elde's disquisition on the Nine Worthy has been much discussed (e.g., Peck (1972), Turville-Petre (1977, 1979), Kiser (1987)). The Worthy first appear in Jacques de Longuyon's *Les Voeux du Paon* (c. 1312), though it is likely that there were earlier accounts of them which have not survived. In the *Voeux,* which was popular in England — there even remain a few lines from an alliterative translation of it, apart from the use Barbour made of it in his *Bruce* (1376) — the poet abruptly interrupts his description of a battle between Alexander and Clarus (see below, note to 339ff.) to say that not even the Nine could compare with Porrus, Clarus' son. The chivalric prowess and glory of Hector, Alexander, and Julius Caesar, Judah Maccabee, Joshua, and David, Arthur, Charlemagne, and Godfrey de Bouillon are then described. This grouping of three pagan, Jewish, and Christian heroes became well known throughout Europe. In Middle English alliterative verse, the Worthy are mentioned in *The Siege of Jerusalem*, *Golagros and Gawain*, and, most notably, in *Morte Arthure* (lines 3250–3455). In some versions, the royal character of the Nine is emphasized. Moran (1978) suggests that aristocratic interest in idealized images of past royalty (common in literature from the North and West Midlands during the second half of the fourteenth century), might explain the Worthy's appearance in *Parlement*. Turville-Petre (1979), however, shows that the Worthy were commonly used to exemplify the vanity of all things and the inevitability of death (see *Morte Arthure*, lines 3452–55).

300   For this account of Hector, besides the *Voeux* (lines 7484–94), the poet probably drew on Guido delle Colonne's *Historia Destructionis Troiae*; there is an alliterative Middle English poem, *The Destruction of Troy*, in which Hector's death is described as well (lines 8643ff.).

308 *nynetene and nyne.* T: *xix and ix*; most editors follow W's *nynety & ix.* and emend to *nynety*. In the *Voeux*, Hector is said to kill nineteen kings and many other people (lines 7484–94).

314–15 The source for Achilles' death is probably Dictys Cretensis' *Ephemeridos belli Troiani* (3.29); see note to line 331.

319 *doun.* T-P emends to *plat*.

322 *serely.* W: *surely;* T-P: *sorely;* G: *sarrely*.

325 *Pantasilia the quene.* G supplies *[prowde]*; followed by T-P.

331 *Dittes and Dares.* Dictys Cretensis and Dares Phrygius both wrote accounts of the Trojan War, which they said were eye-witness reports but which are in fact entirely fictional. They became the chief authorities on the Trojan War in the Middle Ages; Homer was known only second-hand at best.

   demeden. T and T-P: *demedon;* W: *demyn.* G's emendation, followed by O.

332 For Alexander's exploits in defeating the Indian king Porrus and then in capturing Babylon, the poet drew on Longuyon's *Voeux*, which mentions the poisoning of Alexander in Babylon, but departs considerably from the descriptions one finds in the French poem. The poet has incorporated other material from sources unknown to us. Alexander was the subject of two Middle English alliterative poems, *Kyng Alisaunder* and *The Wars of Alexander*, as well as a prose life that translates the same source as the poet of *The Wars* used.

334 *Ercules boundes.* Hercules was thought to have erected two pillars at the straits of Gibraltar, the extreme western verge of the world, where he journeyed to obtain the cattle of Geryon. Alexander's voyage to the Pillars and to the Earthly Paradise (see next note) was well known. See M. M. Lascelles, "Alexander and the Earthly Paradise in Mediaeval English Writings," *Medium Aevum* 5 (1936), 31–47, 79–104, 173–88.

335–36 Enoch and Elias were often pictured as rapt before they died to the Earthly Paradise, where they would remain until the coming of the Antichrist, whom they were supposed to challenge. Dante also mentions Elijah (Elias) in close conjunction with the Hercules' pillars in *Inferno* 26.

338   *Jazon the Grewe.* T: *Iazon the Iewe;* W: *Iosue the Iewe.* W was attempting to make sense of an undoubted confusion that was also in T's exemplar; for *flese of golde,* W reads *slevis of golde.* I accept G's emendation to *Grewe,* "Greek."

339–59   The poet is referring to Alexander's battle against Gadifer of Larris, a leader of the people of Gadres (perhaps Gaza). During his defense of the city, Gadifer was unhorsed and killed by Emenidus. Alexander then joined the battle with his host, which included Emenidus, Sir Filot, and the other knights named in lines 349–52. They were met by Cassamus, Gadifer's brother, who, though an old man, greatly desired to avenge Gadifer's death. Alexander instead took council with Cassamus and persuaded him to make peace with Emenidus. Cassamus told Alexander that Gadifer had two sons, young Gadifer and Betis, whom Clarus, wicked king of Ind, wanted to dispossess; Clarus also wanted to marry Gadifer's daughter Fesonas, much against her will, and had laid siege to Epheson, where all Gadifer's children were. Alexander promised to battle Carrus to make good Emenidus' slaying of Gadifer. There is a Middle English romance of Cassamus.

340   *Gadyfere . . . Gaderayns.* T and T-P: *Godfraye . . . Goderayns.*

356   *hade Fozome.* W and T-P: *hade his fomen.*

360–93   During the seige of Epheson, Clarus' son Porrus was captured but treated with courtesy. One day, while walking in a courtyard, Porrus saw a peacock, which he slew and had prepared for a feast. During the feast, Cassamus proposed that each man make a vow to the peacock; Porrus' vow was to take Emenidus' horse in battle. Baudrain vowed to take Alexander's sword from his own hand, amid all his men. This he does, but is killed by Floridas, one of Alexander's knights. Cassamus vows that if he met Clarus dismounted in battle, he would set him on his horse again, for Porrus' sake, but then slay him. This Cassamus did, which led to his own death at Porrus' hands. The Indians were heartened by this, but ultimately fled before Alexander. Porrus was captured again and chastized by Alexander for his vow; nevertheless, because of his courage in battle, Porrus was treated as a hero. He was allowed to marry Fesonas, who had vowed to marry no one except the man Alexander should choose. Baudrain married Edias, and Betis, Fesonas' brother, married Idores at the same time.

360   *Facron* is the river that flowed through Fozayne (Epheson), line 356.

369   *abaschede.* W: *basshed;* T-P: *baschede.*

371   *kynges.* T-P emends to *beryns.*

389   *bolde Bawderayne of Baderose,* i.e., the bold ruler of Bauderis from Bauderis.

394–404 Alexander's adventures in Babylon are very briefly touched on. His romance with Queen Candace is described in *Kyng Alisaunder* (lines 6648ff.; 7616ff.) and *The Wars of Alexander* (lines 5057ff.).

396   *Candace.* T and T-P: *Candore.* W: *Cadace.*

397   *assayllede.* W: *saylid;* T-P: *sayllede.*

407   *Bruyte.* According to medieval legend, Aeneas' grandson Brutus founded Britain. His name eventually came to stand for any chronicle of British history. Here he seems to be considered an author of one of these chronicles. The poet, as O notes, seems to stress Caesar's connections with Britain to a greater extent than the passages in the *Voeux* do.

408–11   That Caesar built the Tower of London is a long-standing tradition, as is the idea that he built Dover Castle.

414–15   *Romayne.* A province of Rome (?Gaul). (O). Here the poet seems to be following Longuyon, where, as T-P notes (p. 88), "Caesar 'sousmist as Ronmains le roy Cassibilant', *Voeux* 7507." The poet seems unaware that Cassivelaunus was, according to Geoffrey of Monmouth, a British king.

416   *gete hym.* G and O emend to *gete it.* T-P supports T, glossing *gete hym* as "conquered them." W reads *þem.*

426ff.   The poet seems to conflate, if not confuse, the crossing of the Jordan (Joshua 3–4) and the passage through the Red Sea (Ex. 14–16). The stories were linked, even in the Bible. Three French texts of the fifteenth century also make Joshua cross the Red Sea (Turville-Petre, 1979).

442   *Drightynes.* T and T-P: *Drightyn.* G's emendation, followed by O.

443ff. The story of Goliath is in 1 Sam. 17; that of David, Uriah, and Bathsheba in 2 Sam. 11. A similar account of David and Goliath appears in *Morte Arthure* (lines 3416–19); David's conduct with Uriah and Bathsheba is much more starkly presented here than in the *Voeux*.

454ff. The story of Judah Maccabee is in 1 and 2 Maccabees in the Apocrypha.

457 *kynge*. W and T-P: *knyght*.

460 W: *That ful low han be laid of ful long tyme*; G and T-P follow W.

464ff. The account of Arthur in the *Voeux* is very short; it only mentions his battle with the giant Roystone (Ruston), described at lines 481ff., and the encounter on St. Michael's Mount. The poet has added allusions to the Siege Perilous, the names of Arthur's knights, and the battle with Mordred.

470ff. *Sege Perilous*. The Siege Perilous, the seat Merlin made for Arthur. At the start of the Quest for the Holy Grail, letters appear mysteriously inscribed in it that announce that it is reserved for Sir Galahad. In the *Morte Arthure* (lines 3250–3455), Arthur dreams he sees a lady turning a wheel on which there is a silver chair. Six kings have fallen from that chair; two others are climbing toward it. The lady lifts Arthur himself to the seat, gives him gifts, but then turns the wheel, which breaks Arthur's back. The Nine Worthy thus are subject to fortune and the loss of all goods; soon after, Arthur learns of Mordred's betrayal.

476ff. All the knights named were well known in Arthurian legend.

481 *Roystone*. T: *Boystone*; W: *Rusten*. In the *Voeux* the name is Ruiston. Analogues of this story are in the alliterative *Morte Arthure* and the prose *Merlin*.

482 *blyot*. A *bleaunt* is a long embroidered garment. As O observes, the account here is noteworthy in that the giant wants the beards to make a mantle for his bride.

486 *oure kyng*. G supplies *athell* between these words; T-P follows.

497ff. Assuming *Wawayne* is not a scribal alteration for the sake of alliteration — Turville-Petre (1979) thinks, on the evidence of W's *Ewan*, that Ywain is meant

— only here does Arthur bid Gawain throw his sword into the lake; in other versions, it is Lancelot Gyrflet (*Mort Artu*) or Sir Bedivere (*Morte Arthure* and Malory).

502   *Wawayne swith.* O, following W, emends to *Wawayne [start] swith.*

513ff.   The account of Godfrey of Bouillon agrees closely with that in the *Voeux*; only the last line, mentioning Godfrey's death, is new.

520ff.   The account of Charlemagne in the *Voeux* is only nine lines: it says Charles conquered Spain, defeated the Saxons, and reestablished Christianity in Jerusalem. In the *Parlement*, Elde lists the twelve peers, and speaks at greater length of the campaign against the Saxons; he gives a sketchy account of the story of Ferumbras (compare the Middle English translation, *Sir Ferumbras*), and refers to Ganelon's treason and Roland's battle at Roncesvalles, the battle at Saragossa, the siege of Narbonne, and Charlemagne's death at Saint-Denis. All of these events are chronicled in the various French and English romances that deal with Charlemagne's career. The most famous of these is the *Chanson de Roland*.

521   *doussypers.* Originally the twelve peers ("douze pers," "twelve equals") bound to Charlemagne, the term came to designate any illustrious person. The persons mentioned here are Roland, Reiner of Gennes (?Genoa), Oliver (Reiner's son), Aubrey of Burgogne, Ogier the Dane, Naimes of Bavaria, Archbishop Turpin, Tierri the Angevin, Samson, Berard de Mondisdier, Guy of Burgundy, and the four sons of Aymon. "There seems to have been no constant tradition as to the names of the peers, and the list differs almost from text to text" (O, p. 63).

523   T-P follows W for sake of meter: *Olyuer and Aubrye and Ogere the Deannyes.*

529   *knyghtes*, as in G, O, T-P, and W. T: *kynges.*

533   *Salamadyne.* As with Nioles and Maundevyle in lines 539–40, these names have not survived in any other source, although T-P notes that after Charlemagne went to Paderborn, he met the Governor of Barcelona, Suleiman Ibn Al-Araby, with whom he made an alliance.

534   T omits *cité.*

541–47   The story of Sir Ferumbras was the most popular of the Charlemagne romances. T-P gives the following summary: "The giant Saracen, Ferumbras, defeated by Oliver, agrees to be christened. Oliver and other knights are captured and taken over the river Flagot to Mautrible [in Spain], then moved the next day to Aigremont [a Saracen stronghold], where they are imprisoned by Balan, father of Ferumbras. Balan's daughter, Floripas, takes pity on them and rescues them, and hands over the Holy Relics that Ferumbras had taken from Jerusalem. Charlemagne arrives at Aigremont and captures Balan, who refuses to be baptized and so is killed by Ogier. Floripas is baptized, and Charlemagne returns to St Denis with the Holy Relics" (p. 93). A lively version of this narrative appears in Middle English as "The Sultan of Babylon," *Three Middle English Charlemagne Romances*, ed. Alan Lupack (Kalamazoo: Medieval Institute Publications, 1990), pp. 1–103.

546   *Balame.* T-P follows W with *Marchel.* So too in line 548. In lines 558 and 569 he changes *Marchill* to *Balame.* His note explains: "The poet has reversed the names of Balan of the Ferumbras story and Marsile from the *Chanson de Roland.* The scribe, Robert Thornton, who had already transcribed two Charlemagne romances, realized the poet's error and corrected the mistake, but the alliterative patterns and the readings of ms. W reveal what the poet wrote. See Turville-Petre (1974:43n)" (p. 94).

552   *cristened,* as in T and O. W: *halowd;* G and T-P: *fologhed.*

555   *naylede,* as in T and O. T-P: *pynnede;* G: *put.* W inverts word order to read: *was on þe rode naylid.*

558–70   These events are chronicled in the *Chanson de Roland. Merchill* is Marsile, Saracen king of Spain.

570   T omits *hym.*

571–77   The siege of Narbonne is described in a cycle of eight "chansons de geste."

577   *To have and.* T: *To kepe it and.* T-P emends: *To have it and.*

586   In popular medieval tradition, Aristotle and Virgil were both considered masters of all worldly knowing; many legends of their fabulous powers (including their command of alchemy) grew up around them.

588   T-P follows the metrically preferable syntax of W to read: *The grete Alexander to graythe golde when hym lyste.*

593   *blaunchere.* T: *plaunchere.* Literally, a whitener of metals. Compounds of arsenic were used to whiten metals so that they could be transmuted.

594   In the legend referred to, Virgil himself consulted the oracular head he had made when he was about to go on a journey. It said all would be well if Virgil took care of his head. He thought this meant the talking head he had made; on his journey, however, he rode with his head uncovered and died of sunstroke.

       verrayle. T: *vernayle,* or *vervayle.* W: *veryall.* I have adopted G's emendation.

600   As O notes, these books probably are the apocryphal Book of Wisdom and Ecclesiasticus, which were attributed to Solomon in the Middle Ages, rather than Proverbs and Ecclesiastes.

608   *graythed.* T: *graythen.* Galyan appears to be Merlyn's girlfriend, perhaps the Lady of the Lake (?) or an equivalent to Malory's Nyneve.

       kepe. W reads *gete,* which O and T-P follow.

610   *yitt.* Omitted in W; so too in T-P.

614ff.   All the lovers mentioned were famous in the Middle Ages. Although no Middle English romance corresponds to the French *Amadas et Ydoine,* the two lovers are frequently referred to. There are Middle English romances of Ipomadon, Generides, Eglamour, and Tristram and Iseult.

617   *bothe.* T: *boghte.* G's emendation. In favor of *boghte* one might note that although Death does not ordinarily "buy" people, the words are associated; in Lydgate's *Chronicles of Troy* (1430) a character says he will buy honor with his death. *Boghte* can also play on the theological meaning of "redemption."

618   Ipomadon of Apulia marries "La fière" of Calabria; she was called "the haughty one" because she vowed she would only marry the bravest knight in the world.

627   *Candace,* as in G and O. W: *Candore,* and so in T-P.

628   *passed,* as in O and T-P. T: *pasten.* W and G: *passid.*

629   *thay bothen.* W and T-P: *thay all.*

640   T, W, and T-P omit the first *es.*

642   *"For there is no redemption in Hell"* became part of the Office of the Dead.

656   The horn that awakens the dreamer certainly is a hunting horn; in the Middle Ages, Death also was thought to have a summoning trumpet (see Rosemary Woolf, *The English Religious Lyric* [Oxford: Clarendon, 1968], pp. 323, 354); trumpet blasts also were expected to announce the Day of Judgment. See Peck and Turville-Petre, 1977.

Textual Notes

All emendations to the manuscript are listed first; the MS reading follows.

Wynnere and Wastoure

15 hem] hir **64** ther] thre **83** knyghte] kynge **94** gerede full riche] girde in the myddes **121** caughte] caughten **144** bulles] bibulles **157** galegs] galeys **164** balle] balke **166** mayne] maye **176** Be any crafte . . . semyde] *copied after* 185 **186** The ordire . . . I wene] *copied after* 175 **189** Some] Some of **201** wye] wyes demeth] doeth **264** thou] tho **270** rychely] ryhely **288** tynen] tymen **300** freres] it freres **317** itwiste] it wiste **321** se] se es **353** Caudils] *defective to* -ils connynges g *damaged by worm hole* **354** Dariols] *defective to* -oils **355** Mawmene] *defective to* -mene **356** Iche] *defective to* -e **357** That sothe] *defective to* -othe **358** Me tenyth] *defective to* -enyth **359** That iche] *defective to* -he **364** ones] one **372** it] *om.* **390** moste] mothe **411** side] elde **420** wedes] wordes **430** hir] ir *damaged by worm hole* **434** see] fee? **454** hert] *om.* **468** come] *defective from* co- **469** take] *defective* **470** beryinge-daye] *defective from* ber- **471** to holde] *defective* **472** wonne scholde] *defective from* wonn- **473** wyng ther untill] *defective from* wyng **485** sprede] defective from spr- **500** silver] *defective from* sil- **502** kayre] layren

The Parlement of the Thre Ages

1 monethe] monethes **31** of fyve] of v fyve **48** myntid] mytid **69** owte] *om.* **70** slitte] sisilte **84** pawnche] pawche **105** moted] moten **135** semelyeste] semely **147** stiewardes] stiewarde **166** I] *om.* **173** seyde] seyden **180** with] *om.* **184** es] *om.* **233** quopes] quotes **235** Cheres thaym] cheresche hym **252** How thay] how thaire **331** demeden] and demedon **338** Grewe] Iewe **340** Gadyfere] godfraye Gaderayns] goderayns **396** Candace] Candore **416** gete it] gete hym **442** Drightynes] drightyn **446** stong] stongen **481** Roystone] Boystone **502** start] *om.* **511** la Faye] lafaye **529** knyghte] kynges **534** cite] *om.* **570** hym] *om.* **577** have] kepe it **580** nyne] ix nyne **593** blaunchere] plaunchere **594** verrayle] vernayle or vervayle **608** graythed] Graythen **617** now] and now bothe] boughte **618** his] hir **627** Candace] Candore **628** passed] pasten **640** es] *om.*

Glossary

als *as, when, while*
ames *plans*
are *before*
aughte *obtained, ruled*
awnn *own*

banke(s), bonke *bank, slope, hillside*
bent *battlefield*
beryn(e) *knight, nobleman, man, servant, judge*
betyde *come to pass*
ble(e) *color*
bown(ne) *ready, prepared*
brande, bronde *sword*
brayde, brauden, brouden *link(ed), embroider(ed), raise, flourish*

can, kane, ken *know*
cayre, kayre(n) *ride*
couthe *could*

delyn *divide, deal, distribute, fight, concern (oneself) with*
dreped, drepide, drepit *slew*
dynttis *blows*

eghe, eghne *eye, eyes*
es *is*
ever(r)ous *eager*

fare *prosperity*
fawkon *falcon*
felde *field, battlefield*
fele *many*
fere *wife, companion*
festes *feasts*
fete *feet, talons*
fey *fated to die*

fole *fool*
fongen *get, take, capture, seize*
forthi *therefore, wherefore, accordingly*
founden *hasten*

gate *way, path*
gome *man, warrior*
graythe *prepare*

hathelle *man, knight*
hedir *hither*
hedis *heads*
heghe *high*
hem *them*
hent *seize*
here *hear;* herde *heard*
here *army*
here *hair*
hert *heart*
hete, highte *assure, promise, order*
hoven *wait, be poised*

iche *each, every*
ichone *each one*

kayre *ride, return*
ken *know, introduce, direct*
kythe *make known, reveal;* kyd(de), kiddeste *(most) known*
kythe *country, people*

lache *get, take;* laughte *took*
launde *glade*
lede *man;* ledys *men*
lygge, lyes *remain, rest*

nayt(t)ly *exactly, fittingly*
neghe *near, nigh; approach; nearly, soon*

81

nerre *nearer*
nother *none other*

ogh *ought, own, owe;* forms: **owethe, owthe, aughte**
one *on*
one *one, a certain*
one *alone, only*
ones *once*
or *before*

paramour(e)s *passionately, lovers*
paye *please, pay*

raylede *arrayed, decorated*
rechen *give, reach, pay;* **raughte(n)** *grasped, extended*
renke *knight, man*
rewme *realm, kingdom*
rewthe *pity*
rowte *company*

sadde *firm, heavy, serious*
segge *man*
se(e)re *diverse, separate*
serely *individually, separately*
sexe *six*
siche *such*
sone *at once*
sothe *true, truth*
swith, swythe *soon, quickly*
sythen *since, then, after*

tene, tenyn *annoy, harass*
thaire *their*
the *thee, you*
thies *these*
triste *trusty*
trouthe *troth, plighted word*

upbrayde *take up*

wayte *guard, keep, watch, observe*

wele *wealth, goods, happiness*
wende *go, turn;* **wiendes** 3 sg. pr., **wend** 2 pl. pr., **went** I sg. pa., **wentten** 3 pl., **wende** imper. sg.
werlde *world*
w(i)ete *know, learn;* forms: **wot(e)** I. sg. pr., **wate** 2 sg. pr., **wiete** 3 sg. pr. subj., **wiste** I & 3 sg. pa.
witt *mind, thought, intelligence, guile, craft*
wonne *dwell, remain, linger*
worthe(n) *become, be*
wriche *wretch*
wy *man*

yeris *years*
yerne *readily, faithfully*
yette *surrender*
yolden *surrendered, yielded*
ynewe *enough*